Luanne Botta is a seasoned lea⟨ "Linksters," Generation Z, whic⟨ generation. Luanne is a voice crying in the wilderness, calling them to freedom, holiness, fidelity to God and to the Judeo-Christian worldview. Her anointed message is penetrating and timely. There has never been a generation more at risk nor has there ever been a more timely message.

—*Richard Nugara Ph.D.*
Adjunct Professor of Divinity,
Biblical Studies and Christian Ministry
Regent University, Virginia Beach, VA

The Warrior Within is insightful and spiritually convicting. Luanne's experience as a high school teacher gives her a true understanding of the spiritual battles young men face in our world today. She charges young men to recognize the deception of our current culture and counter it with the truth of God's mighty Word!

—*Pat Kenney, BSN*

Young men grow up surrounded by temptation and in a culture permeated with sex and violence. The world has no answers. Luanne Botta's new book, *The Warrior Within*, addresses biblical principles to equip men of all ages to fight against the onslaught trying to strip them of their masculinity and purity. Luanne has a proven track record ministering to and helping teenagers, including young men, overcome their personal struggles. This book is a must read for both young men and parents alike.

—*Reverend Gary Mitrik*
Senior Pastor, Greater Works Outreach
Monroeville, Pennsylvania

You can't say the name Luanne Botta without getting a big smile on your face and a surge of blood into your heart. Her sweet vivacious personality is contagious and you will be captivated by the message of wisdom and love she will convey to all who have ears to hear. Teens are one of her specialties and truth is her message.

Luanne is my forever friend! Fifteen of my thirty years of teaching was side by side with her and we were partners in crime, exposing to our students the enemies plan to turn their eyes toward the world, while the Lord's plan was to turn their eyes upon Jesus. Five of my children had Luanne as a teacher and will sing along with the other hundreds she has taught that "she was the best of all the rest."

The Warrior Within is not just another book out there, but it is a priceless handbook for teenage boys. I even suggest that parents read it as it will help you raise Godly sons.

—*Patty Samuels*
English Teacher/Guidance Counselor

There is a battle happening each and every day in the world. Most people don't see it, but this spiritual battle is one that needs an increased number of first rate soldiers. One who will not be tripped up before they can even stand to fight. This book gives us the step by step directions each man needs to follow so that they are ready not only to fight, but to overcome. "Miss Botta" (Luanne) has been preaching this message for decades and those that listen find hope. I highly recommend this book to every young man.

—*Jonathan Curry*
Teaching Pastor
Children's/ Married Couples Pastor
Greater Works Outreach
Monroeville, Pennsylvania

Luanne speaks truth from a biblical standpoint that brings freedom and liberty. God has used her as a watchman for today's generation in directing young men and women to the truth of the Scriptures, pointing them to Jesus and helping them to break free from the lies of this world. *The Warrior Within* is a timely book with relevant topics and should be read by all young men!

—*Diane Snyder*
Science Teacher/Guidance Counselor

As parents, Luanne Botta is our "go-to-author." Her keen ability to reach the younger generation, coupled with godly insights and wisdom, makes Luanne's counsel to teens invaluable!

Her first book, *Young Hearts Pure Lives*, met our teenage daughter right where she and her friends find themselves—in a culture spinning out of control. Now, and right on time in the intensifying teenage culture, Luanne takes her same boldness to challenge young men to walk in the standard God has set for them. Luanne is not afraid to confront issues young men deal with that are often unaddressed. She uses biblical principles to expose the distorted messages young men receive from their peers, the media and from within. Luanne's book carries a necessary "tough love" message that will change the course of young men's lives. She will encourage them to embrace their true identity, to embrace the God who calls them and to embrace *The Warrior Within*.

—*Linda and Tim Hart*
Parents Fighting the Battle
Parents Standing for Truth

Luanne Botta has done it again, and this time, young men get to benefit as she both challenges and encourages them. Over the years, I have personally witnessed Luanne's work with young women as a speaker, counselor, and writer. Now, in her newest book, *The Warrior Within*, she comes alongside young men to help them "stand strong" as she uses God's Word to promote a healthy, Christian view of sexuality for men. I am delighted to recommend this book for male "warriors" to help them *"fight the good fight"* (1 Timothy 6:12.)

—*Douglas J. Carson*
Supervising Principal
Beaver County Christian School
Beaver County, PA

THE
WARRIOR
WITHIN

YOUNG MEN STANDING STRONG IN A RECKLESS WORLD

LUANNE BOTTA

ISBN: 978-1-64123-294-4
eBook ISBN: 978-1-64123-293-7

Printed in the U.S.A.
Copyright © 2019 by Luanne Botta

Published by
Whitaker House
1030 Hunt Valley Circle
New Kensington, PA 15068

Unless otherwise indicated, Scripture quotations used in this book are from the *Holy Bible, New International Version*® NIV © 1973, 1978, 1984 by International Bible Society. Used by Permission of Zondervan Publishing House. All rights reserved.

Scripture quotations marked (NASB) are taken from the *New American Standard Bible*®, © 1960, 1962, 1963, 1968, 1971, 1972, 1973, 1975, 1977, 1988 by The Lockman Foundation. Used by Permission.

Edited by Vicki Mlinar

www.luannebotta.com

Special thank you to Margaree Pertle,

Thank you for your steadfast encouragement for me to continue with God's call on my life when there seemed to be no reason to hold on. I would never have stayed in ministry without your assurance to not quit. Your warm heart and friendship is a great treasure to me. I am encouraged by your strength, integrity and daily fight.

You truly are a warrior of the faith!

FOREWORD

I met Luanne Botta my senior year of high school. I remember meeting her and thinking, wow, now here is a teacher that loves students; she's the real deal. Even when I was in the midst of my struggles with drugs and sin, she still believed in me and encouraged me to follow the gifts that God had put in my life.

After I received Christ my senior year, I remember having many talks in our Bible class about purity. Most of the male students were struggling in this area. Many of the students could be vulnerable and honest in Luanne's class. We were able to find strength and hope; we remained pure in the midst of a world that tells us different.

I believe that through those open and honest talks, the students were able to receive clarity, and also receive the tools to engage in the battle of purity within.

It's time for us as a group of men to rise up and begin to stand—begin to become the Lead-Hers we were meant to be. It's time for us to get real, in order to get right. I encourage you, as you read this book, look through it with the eyes of faith and believe that things can and will change.

The world tells us that we have to act, look and be a certain way, but Luanne gives you the knowledge to make it through the tough times. This book, *The Warrior Within*, will help you find freedom and discover what real strength of purity looks like in your day to day life.

—*Pastor Shawn Collins*
Bridge City Church
East Liberty, Pennsylvania

CONTENTS

TERMS AND DEFINITIONS

Abstain	to refrain from something; to hold back.
Adultery	voluntary sexual intercourse with another person other than your spouse.
Celibacy	the state of not being married; abstaining from sexual intercourse.
Character	qualities or features that distinguish one person from another; moral ethical strength; reputation.
Desensitized	non-reactive; insensitive, callous, numb.

Fornication	consensual sexual intercourse between two persons not married to each other.
Immoral	conscienceless of moral principles; what is right.
Innuendo	to hint, allusion, insinuation, not straight forward.
Integrity	honest, high standards of morals and values.
Moral	capable of making the distinction between right and wrong in conduct.
Pornography	material (such as books or photographs) that depict erotic behavior and is intended to cause sexual excitement.
Promiscuous	sexual intercourse with many persons, without plan or purpose; casual.
Respect	to consider worthy of high regard; held in honor or high esteem.
Responsible	accountable; obligation.
Virtuous	moral excellence; value; right action and thinking.

INTRODUCTION

Gentlemen,

I am privileged to write this book for you. I hope you understand it is to strengthen, encourage and challenge you to be the man God has called you to be. Not a perfect man, but a man that trusts and believes his God.

May I say first and foremost, you have a voice in this culture! A culture that is literally spinning out of control. Your voice is crucial for your generation. Your voice is not about your opinion. Your voice is needed to speak truth. The truth scares many people, especially those who want to live life their own way. But being a warrior within and a warrior for your generation, it is imperative that you understand the fight. I am very aware that many of you come from different backgrounds. These truths apply to everyone, no matter where or how you have grown up.

It is time to discover God's direct plan and path for you to help you be that voice of truth. We will consider many things: how the media is selling seduction to capture your mind and heart through pornography; wisdom in friendships; the girls in your life; the battle of sexting; becoming the warrior within. Most of this book is going to speak candidly about sexual integrity God's way. (I know you just rolled your eyes!) There has been so much garbage from the culture thrown at you for years regarding this one topic, and it is necessary to be up front and honest about it.

I was a teacher at a private Christian school for seventeen years. I have reached out to many of those former male students along with my own nephews to help give you wisdom, advice, encouragement and a call to stay strong in this culture. Some of these guys are single, one is a recent college graduate, some are married, some are married with kids, some have kids out of the house already. But all speak with great wisdom and encouragement to you as a young man looking to be the man God has called you to be for your generation. Take what they say seriously. They have already gone before you. They know exactly what you are dealing with. They know the hopes, the dreams, the struggles, and the urgent message that you were called, at a time like this, to be the leader and voice for your generation.

As a "man after God's heart," you will be challenged and encouraged to live your life differently from your friends in the world regarding the opposite sex. In becoming that warrior within, you must understand the battle that is raging over you in this one topic of sexual desire.

You probably have noticed since you were a little boy, that girls love the "happily ever after" fairytale. While you were playing with cars, trucks and making a gun out of anything you could get your hands on, they were playing with baby dolls, dress up, and house. They want to be swept off their feet by that knight in shining armor. An impossible task without understanding who you are and Whose you are and the role the Lord has placed on your life as a man of God. In this study, I want to give you that perspective through the Word of God and through other men's experiences so that you can live the life you were designed to live by your Creator and to love the adventure you were given.

So, as you dive into this book, I know I may step on a few toes, but it is to be honest with you about where you might be heading in your life – places that are not good for you. I know some of you may have already fallen to sexual sin, and you need a safe place to start again. Some of you may be in a sexual relationship now and find nothing wrong with it. Hopefully, you will discover that God has a different way for you. He wants you to know He is not keeping anything *from* you, He is keeping something *for* you. Others of you are standing in great strength and courage, waiting on the Lord from a clean and pure heart.... He loves all of you so much.

Gentlemen, when the Lord sees you, He sees you strong, forgiven, loved, gifted, His son, a warrior, a leader, a success in Him with whatever you put your hand to and so much more—you just need to grab a hold of that. So many people are looking for a title for their lives: a great athlete, a computer wiz, the comedian of the class, the best friend. However, the greatest title you could ever achieve and strive for is to be "a man after God's own heart."

So..., I put before you a study that will challenge and direct your life to that *Warrior Within* and all that God has called you to be in this day and hour you are walking through. Again, it is a privilege to speak life and wholeness to your heart and spirit through the Word of God and the words of this book. And as Marlin, Nemo's dad, says appropriately and perfectly in the last line of *Finding Nemo*, "Go have an adventure, son!"

THAT ADVENTURE CAN START NEW TODAY!

Do you not know? Have you not heard? The LORD is the everlasting God, the Creator of the ends of the earth. He will not grow weary and his understanding no one can fathom. He gives strength to the weary and increases the power of the weak. Even youths grow tired and weary, and young men stumble and fall; but those who hope in the LORD will renew their strength. They will soar on wings like eagles; they will run and not grow weary, they will walk and not be faint.
—Isaiah 40:28–31

GOD'S PLAN. GOD'S PATH. GOD'S TIME.

"Trust in the LORD with all your heart and lean not on your own understanding; in all your ways acknowledge him, and he will make your paths straight."
—Proverbs 3:5–6

I have chosen to open this book with a quote from Tim Tebow:

"My mom used to quote Isaiah 64:4 about waiting on the Lord. It doesn't mean being complacent. It means understanding that He has a plan, and that we're not the ones in control. In the meantime, we need to strive to use our gifts and abilities fully."

We have all watched Tim's life so far, how he has always unashamedly confessed faith in Jesus. We have watched him walk through great disappointment to not play in the NFL after being so incredibly successful playing for the University of Florida and a Heisman Trophy winner, the greatest individual award in college football. He had to learn to wait and be patient for the new path, plan, and timing of the Lord to play out over his life. He has had to do that in front of millions of people. Amid sarcasm and criticism, he stands his ground, trust and waits upon his God.

This first chapter is to reiterate to you that same God has a plan, path, time and purpose for your life. I know you have heard that all of your life, but it's actually true. You are not here by chance. Your story is written by the Creator of the Universe. Think about that. The story of your life is penned by the Most High God. I don't know what that means to you, but one thing it should say to you is that you have been chosen, picked out by God to walk this earth for as many years as He has ordained for you in a manner that will give Him glory and you pleasure. There is a purpose and a plan that is fit just for you in the very heart of God. No matter how you see yourself right now, the Lord sees you as a mighty man of valor in His eyes. This chapter will hopefully begin to show you that.

I am reminded of the story in Judges 6 regarding Gideon. He seemed to think very lowly of himself, thinking he couldn't do what God was calling him to do. Look at how God sees him, compared to how he sees himself.

When the angel of the LORD appeared to Gideon, he said, "The LORD is with you, mighty warrior." —Judges 6:12

He was telling Gideon that what He saw in him and called him to do, he could do it as the Lord was with him. Gideon questions the Lord wondering why all these bad things were happening to him and Israel his people. Questioning God's goodness, saying He had abandoned them and their situation.

The Lord responds to these questions:

Go in the strength you have and save Israel out of Midian's hand. Am
I not sending you?"   —Judges 6:14

God did not answer Gideon's questions as He knew Gideon's faith was small. What the Lord does do is tell him to go in strength. The Lord was telling him what he saw in Gideon...a man of strength. Then God gives Gideon a question: *"Am I not sending you?"* Trying to convince Gideon that he is not alone in this battle, He was sending him...the Lord is with him. Gideon responds:

"But Lord, Gideon asked, "How can I save Israel? My clan is the
weakest in Manasseh, and I am the least in my family."

"AM I NOT SENDING YOU?"

Doesn't Gideon sound like all of us? I can't do it. I'm not good enough. I don't have what it takes. I'm scared. I'm young. This culture is too much for just my voice. You chose the wrong guy.

The Lord responds:

"I will be with you, and you will strike down all the Midianites together."

The Lord is constantly reassuring Gideon that He is with him and won't let him go as he walks out his journey in the Lord. As God was with this young man, Gideon, so he is with you.

You have been called by God to be a man of valor for your generation. Valor meaning – boldness, especially in battle; heroic courage; bravery. In walking out the warrior within you, you, like Gideon, might feel so far away from being that warrior, that man of valor. Thinking that you don't have what it takes to be this young man of courage when the entire culture is screaming at you with a different voice and a different way of living. But you, my friend, have what it takes to be the warrior God sees. You may have small faith right now in yourself, but Gideon also was a young man being called out to do great things for the Lord and his faith was also small. But God used him anyway as He will use you. As you journey through your high school years, I inspire and encourage you to reach the goal of being this man of valor, the warrior within.

HOW TO GET STARTED

I want to begin with this encouragement from my friend Mark. It is a very powerful way to get started in this journey. It is called the "5-second decisions." It will give you a good way to begin thinking about when you are in certain situations in your life and how to take that 5 seconds before you respond. Here is Mark:

> Every day we all have "5-second decisions" that can become defining moments in how our lives turn out. For example, lying in bed when the alarm goes off in the morning we can think "jump up and get to the gym" or "snooze for another 15 minutes." It's the decision between drinking a tall glass of water or a sugary Coco Cola, or even a more difficult decision to choose between going to that party that you know will offer many temptations or heading out to a movie with friends instead…these decisions compounded over time will create very different results in our lives. The "5-second decision" is the hard part, beyond that it's really not that difficult. In fact, we feel better and are better when we make the right decisions. As a young person, you often tend to think less about these types of decisions because you aren't thinking of "the end" of your lives and how you can shape it. Our culture today programs you to "do it if it feels good," "do what you want to do," "it's ok everybody is doing it." I have learned as I reflect on my days as a teenager, and now having observed my own children go through this process, that if it's the popular thing to do, the easy or the comfortable thing to do, it's very likely not the right thing to do, nor will it lead to blessings in your lives. Most of the "easy decisions" that satisfy your flesh will lead to disappointment and destruction. The peer pressure today to engage in pre-marital sex, to underage

drink, or get involved with drugs is very real, and stronger than ever, but each opportunity brings about a "5-second decision" on your part that will lead you down one path or another...at any age.

You can be a person that pushes through those tough decisions with His help ("*I can do all things through Christ who strengthens me.*" Phillipians 4:13). You can be the one our young generation looks up to as someone who stands for something and doesn't fall for anything. Success looks different to different people. I want to encourage you to associate with others who share the desire to do the right thing, to stay accountable, to be a light in a very dark world. This association is 90 percent of the battle – it could save your life and the lives of others. Daily renew your mind by learning what the Word of God teaches about purity, grace and forgiveness. He has great plans for you! ("*For I know the plans I have for you, declares the Lord, plans to prosper you and not harm you, plans to give you a hope and a future.*" – Jeremiah 29:11). If you have made some wrong decisions to this point, you can overcome those, and through the grace of Christ get back on the right track and be a testimony of His grace and forgiveness. I would like to personally challenge you to be different, be a good example, and succeed. Our world today needs you. You can do it!

Mark

This is so good...the "5-second decisions" in your life. Those will be the decisions you make. And like Mark said, the hard part is making that "5-second decision." That decision over the situation in your life that is presented to you in a moments time. You will be challenged throughout your life to make decisions. Some you will make wisely, some will not be too wise and you will need to learn from them and sometimes go back and fix them. We all have to do this. But if you can keep this "5-second decision" idea before you, you will be way ahead of the game to make better decisions for yourself. What a great tool to live by.

GOD'S PLAN AND PATH REGARDING SEXUAL INTEGRITY

Like I said in the Introduction section, most of this book is going to be about sexual integrity the way God intended it to be. It is not intended to condemn, sex is not the unpardonable sin. But from listening to teens for many, many years, it is the one topic they are most burdened by and most broken with. Please understand that God had a plan from the very beginning concerning sex and His plan was solely in the context of marriage. One man and one woman. Why? Because God's intention was to bring two people together, a man and a woman, and they were going to become one, forming a bond and a covenant that was to last a life time. Outside of that bond, sex is causing broken hearts, shattered relationships, insecurity, disease, emotional heartache (yes, guys you do have emotions), and broken fellowship from the very heart of God. *"For this reason a man will leave his father and mother and be united to his wife"* (Mark 10:7).

Let me reassure you and say this right from the beginning...sex is good. (I just saw your eyes get real big!) The Lord wants you to enjoy it, it's how He designed it, but He gives the boundaries in marriage...in the context of marriage. Which is His plan and His best for you. It was His idea from the beginning. It's not MTV's idea or the BET station's idea...it was God's idea from the start. And He calls it good. The culture has perverted it in so many ways making it seem dirty and impure. It was never meant to be tainted the way the culture has abused it.

HE GIVES THE BOUNDARIES IN MARRIAGE

See if this analogy makes sense...Do you want to go to college? What do you have to do to get to the college of your choice? I'm suspecting you said yes to the first question. The answer to the second question is your grades 9th–12th grade will dictate what college you get into. If you choose to blow off studying in 9th and 10th grade, you won't be able to catch up with a GPA that will get you into that school of your choice. I watched it happen so many times as a teacher. You have to have good grades to get into that school you always wanted to go to. Your grades follow you.

I have another question: Do you want to get married one day? I'm going to guess the majority of you said yes since that's the answer I get speaking in front of students. I know you are not thinking about marriage right now in your life and you may wait well into your 20s to marry, so if you said yes, what are you going to do with all of these years in between that time? What are you doing that will help you to have a good, strong and healthy relationship/marriage with this beauty you will pursue? You are not too young to be planning for that. Some of you will find this girl you are looking for in college. Well, what's your plan now? Are you going to give her your heart, or pieces of your heart because you gave yourself away to so many other girls before you met her? Fella's—you have a great future ahead of you. I think the following information may help you...

In finding this beauty to rescue as part of your adventure with God, you need to be very aware that she is a gift. She is God's gift first, and He is willing to give her to you. Look at what the Lord says about this gift, and notice where your role is...this covenant is to be:

+ **treasured.** *"He who FINDS a wife, finds a good thing and obtains favor from the Lord"* (Proverbs 18:22 NASB).

Notice the word find—it means "to meet along the way." When you are serious about having a godly woman to love and cherish...watch how the Lord puts her in your path. Notice also that finding a wife is a good thing and you obtain favor from the Lord. He calls it good and gives you favor as his son and daughter.

What this verse does NOT say is, "He who finds someone to sleep with finds a good thing and obtains favor; or he who has sex with as many girls as he wants finds favor; or he who uses a girl to get his needs met is a good thing and has favor with God." You know I could go on and on with this. No, it says, "He who finds a WIFE, finds a good thing and obtains favor from the Lord." What needs to change in the way you are conducting yourself to get to this place of being a man God can trust with one of His daughters?

+ **protected.** *"Husbands, love your wives, just as Christ also loved the church and gave himself up for her"* (Ephesians 5:25 NASB).

Once again, you have a mandate from the Lord, to love your wife as Christ loved the church. To protect and honor her. Women want to feel safe and secure with their husbands. You have been called by God

– to protect her. What an honor and privilege of an assignment from the very heart of God. As I said earlier, I know you may not be thinking about marriage right now, but you can use these principles on how you will date in this season of your life. How to make her feel protected and honored.

+ **enjoyed.** *"Enjoy life with the woman whom you love..."* (Ecclesiastes 9:9 NASB).

God is not a kill joy. He wants you to enjoy your life. Your youth. You have a whole life ahead of you...when you keep things in the perspective of being a man after God's heart looking for an adventure of a life time on His terms...you will find great enjoyment with so many things in your life.

GOD IS NOT A KILL JOY.

+ **held with great commitment.** *"Marriage is to be held in honor among all, and the marriage bed is to be undefiled"* (Hebrews 13:4 NASB).

There it is again...the "marriage" bed, not just anyone's bed, couch, game room...but the marriage bed. Undefiled meaning "free from stain or blemish; uncorrupted." There is much that I want to talk about on this topic of defiled...it will be in another chapter. But there is a commitment to be married...a covenant.

+ **handled with the Word of God.** *"So husbands ought also to love their own wives as their own bodies"* (Ephesians 5:28 NASB).

There is so much instruction, especially in the book of Ephesians, for you as a potential husband and how you are to treat your wife and kids. I'm telling you, if you live your life according to the Word of God, things will not be perfect because nothing is, you will have ups and downs, but they will be fulfilling for you in a way that will bring you joy.

You see, God has the *best plan* concerning relationships and sex. Through this study, please embrace His truths and allow the Holy Spirit to reprogram your mind away from what the world is conveying to you about sex and relationships. God is in the business of working things out for your good and His glory. He promised that **if you** *"trust in the* LORD *with all your heart and lean not on your own understanding; and in all your ways acknowledge him, and he will make your paths straight"* (Proverbs 3:5–6). It is His promise to you, see the encouragement it brings that He is in control of your life and He is directing it as you allow Him to.

SINCE THE BEGINNING OF TIME

Let's go a little deeper here and see God's intentions since time began. In the second chapter of Genesis, life in the Garden was good! Adam and Eve could eat freely from all God had given them. In that freedom, there was pure love, contentment, joy, no fear, no shame, peace, oneness with God, laughter, rest, no anxiety...the list could go on and on. They were enjoying each other, they were having fun with each other and they knew God like no one in the world will ever have the opportunity to know Him, without sin. They were living in obedience to what God says leads to life.

God made a binding agreement, a promise that maintained a relationship with Adam and Eve. In that covenant, they were His children in His image. He promised never to leave or forsake them, and He promised to be their God. He never wanted that relationship to be broken or hindered in any way. But in their disobedience, Adam and Eve insisted on listening to the voice of Satan and his accusations against what God had clearly said. Then emotional, physical, and spiritual death entered the world.

This is exactly what God has done with you; He made a covenant with you, claiming you as His own. God wants you to enjoy the life that He has given you here on earth. He wants you to walk in the gifts and relationships He places before you.

You must be very wise at your age and aware of the voices of opposition that are contrary to what God is saying. This is especially vital when dealing with relationships with the opposite sex.

Let's go further.

CONSEQUENCES OF DISOBEDIENCE

In the third chapter of Genesis, Satan despised what God called good, questioning the truthfulness of His Word. We must understand Satan's way of deception that Eve missed here.

It says in Genesis 3:6, "*When the woman saw that the fruit of the tree was good and pleasing to the eye, and also desirable for gaining wisdom, she took some and ate it.*" Notice—she saw, she took, and she ate. After reasoning with the voice of deception in her mind, she decided to reach out and grab the lie, taste, and eat. Then it says, "*she gave also to her husband, who was with her, and he ate it.*" What caused Adam not to stand in obedience to what God said and instead join his wife in denying and disobeying what God had asked? Think about it.

You might think, "Well, that was stupid, God had given them so much." All He asked them not to touch was that one tree. Yet they were enticed away to their own desires. But think about it, God has given your generation so much as well. He wants you to grow up whole and healthy in your heart and mind, without crazy insecurity or fear or rejection regarding relationships. He says that it will cause some problems in your life, your heart. Yet take a look around your generation…they see, they take, and they eat anyhow.

How is this any different from what Adam and Eve did? Think about that. Because of this disobedience, and just as God had warned, sin and the consequences of sin entered the world.

SPIRITUAL BROKENNESS

You need to understand—and maybe some of you are experiencing this right now—sex is not just physical but emotional, mental, and spiritual. We forget that spiritual death can occur when we are walking in disobedience to God's will. There may be nothing that lays more heavily on us than when we are in Christ but feel the depth of a separation in that relationship.

Many times, sin causes us to withdraw from God. You can allow your thoughts to be so riddled with lust, impure motives, impure thoughts, so over-saturated with pornography and books with sexual scenes and content that your mind becomes tainted and unclean. This causes a breach between you and God. (We will address the deep issue of pornography in another chapter).

Spiritual brokenness brings about not only a broken relationship with God but the loss of one's ability and desire to please or seek Him. This can cause you to do your own thing and live in the wilderness of broken fellowship with God. It's not that He has left you, but the sin you carry has caused a breach between the two of you. Don't let your heart be imprisoned to this kind of disobedience. He is calling you back to Himself.

SEX IS NOT JUST PHYSICAL BUT EMOTIONAL, MENTAL, AND SPIRITUAL.

GOD OUR RESCUER

God has come to rescue His own, which is you. All that was once made so perfect in the Garden has become tainted. Because God loves, accepts, cherishes, and has made a covenant with you, He hasn't left you in this state of sin. His mercy and His Father's heart toward you have once and for all rescued you from eternal sin and death through the sacrifice and the shedding of the blood of His own Son, Jesus Christ. Through Jesus' death and resurrection, you are free to go to Him and be renewed; the separation or breach in relationship is completely gone through true repentance and forgiveness. He calls you to this freedom...

> How can a young man keep his way pure? By keeping it according to Your word. With all my heart I have sought You; do not let me wander from Your commandments. Your word I have treasured in my heart, that I may not sin against You. —Psalm 119:9-11 (NASB)

What great news to know that you have been rescued...and what a great warrior your Lord truly is!

This is why you need to adhere to what you learn in this study of God's plan for your life regarding relationships and sex. There is so much involved. It's about valuing and respecting your role as a man of God. It's about desiring to be whole in Christ long before you go looking for love. It's about being confident in who you are and Whose you are. You want His best…His plan…His path…His time.

He is completely for you. You are always on His heart and mind. (*"How precious to me are your thoughts, O God! How vast is the sum of them! Were I to count them, they would outnumber the grains of sand. When I awake, I am still with you"* Psalm 139:17–18.) He wants you to see His heart in this matter regarding sexual integrity and His plans for you. And He knows you will fall many times, we all do, but He is right there to rescue you and get you back up on your feet again. That's what a warrior does.

HE IS COMPLETELY FOR YOU.

Below are some truths from God's Word to help you solidify your understanding that He has a plan and a path and has you in mind when He spoke these words of truth!

MAKING GOD'S CASE THROUGH HIS WORD

"For I know the plans I have for you," declares the Lord, *"plans to prosper you and not to harm you, plans to give you hope and a future."*
—Jeremiah 29:11

I know all of you are very familiar with this verse, but read it again.

This is a very personal Scripture. Do you see how God says, "I know," "I have," and "for you"? Do you believe He has a plan for your life? Does God have good or bad plans? Is His future for you a disaster, or one full of hope?

You must rest assured that God had your days written down before even one of them came to be (see Psalm 139:16, *"…all the days ordained for me were written in your book before one of them came to be"*). Trust Him through this time of decisions: what friends (guys and girls) you are to link arms with; where to go to college; what career/ministry you should pursue. He has the plan, and He wants to reveal it to you piece by piece. Take the time to sit before Him and begin to listen for direction, guidance, and for all He has in store. His plans are good: to bring you a bright future filled with great hope!

> There is an appointed time for everything. And there is a time for every event under heaven. —Ecclesiastes 3:1 (NASB)

There absolutely is a time and season for everything in life. If you push for *your* timetable, instead of God's, on events in your life, you can cause real havoc.

God brought Eve to Adam. The timing for each of you in this area will be different. Allow God to work things out for you in His way and His time. You will see that He always knows exactly what He is doing.

Listen carefully: the word "time" in this Scripture means "divinely appointed." So, if you let Him, God will divinely appoint the timeframe of you meeting her. Waiting on that time frame is what makes things difficult. But when you are confident that God has a divinely appointed time, you can relax, enjoy this season of your life – there are so many great friends and great memories that can be made right now without the pressure of having a relationship or sex with someone who was never God's plan for your life.

> Do not arouse or awaken love until it so desires.
> —Song of Solomon 2:7

This Scripture is repeated two other times in the Song of Solomon (3:5 and 8:4), and it is always in the context of physical intimacy. It is a charge and a challenge to the daughters of the King. It is saying loud and clear—don't arouse love or awaken love until the proper time. I wanted you to see this.

As a young man, you are not to pressure a girl with your sexual desire. When you arouse or awaken the physical part of a relationship, it will cause you to make unwise decisions that your flesh and feelings can't handle. Plus, once that door is opened, it is very difficult to go back.

You are being charged and challenged today to walk with integrity in your relationship with girls and not awaken desire that should not be fulfilled outside the marriage bed. This is going to take great discipline and sacrifice on your part in this season of your life *until* the proper time has been divinely ordained by the Lord, which is in marriage.

For this is the will of God, your sanctification; that is, that you abstain from sexual immorality; that each of you know how to possess his own vessel in sanctification and honor, not in lustful passion, like the Gentiles who do not know God; and that no man transgress and defraud his brother in the matter because the Lord is the avenger in all these things, just as we also told you before and solemnly warned you. For God has not called us for the purpose of impurity, but in sanctification. Consequently, he who rejects this is not rejecting man but the God who gives His Holy Spirit to you. —1 Thessalonians 4:3-8 (NASB)*

Everyone wants to know what the will of God is. It is always such a popular question. When it comes to sexual integrity, God's will is written out so clearly in this Scripture. In fact, it gives you the exact answer: abstain from sexual immorality. Kind of clear don't you think?

This includes your thoughts, what you are thinking when you see a girl walk by you. Your eyes, where are your eyes focusing on her? Sexual integrity is the whole person.

SEXUAL INTEGRITY IS THE WHOLE PERSON.

This Scripture also says not to defraud your brother in the matter. Defraud in this context means "take advantage of." Some girls take advantage of you as a guy by the way they dress, not realizing what it does to your thought life. And some guys take advantage of girls who choose to offer parts of their body to you in any manner. Which includes sexting, which we will talk about in another chapter. To reject this truth is not rejecting man, but rejecting God and His will for your life.

That's why He gives you direct answers to this question of His will for your life.

Flee from sexual immorality. All other sins a man commits are outside his body, but he who sins sexually sins against his own body.
—1 Corinthians 6:18

Flee sexual immorality. Again, another challenge. To flee is to *run*. To do a 180-degree turn and run! It is so specific here that those who sin sexually sin against their own bodies. Pretty amazing, isn't it? We do this to ourselves simply because we desire our own way.

Once again, God created sex to be a beautiful and essential part of marriage. Outside of the marriage bed, it always hurts someone. Spiritually, it can affect your walk with the Lord. It can affect you emotionally causing depression and discouragement. Through disease, it most certainly can affect you physically. That's why it says to flee, run from sexual sin.

On TV, in movies, and in music, sex outside of marriage is treated as normal and the family unit is treated as odd. But we all know that sexual sin can devastate families, ministries, nations, and the best of friends. God knows that the consequences of sex outside of marriage are costly, and He desires that we not get caught in the grip of its trap. Trust His truth in this matter.

LOOK ONE MORE TIME!

So you see, it's time to claim or reclaim your integrity and your relationship with God, even when it is not popular in our culture or among your peers to do so. I trust that, through this study, you will have a new attitude about your value in God, about having a clean heart and a pure mind, and about setting boundaries to protect what is yours until the woman God brings into your life commits her life to you at the altar.

I know that waiting until marriage is a very, very unpopular message especially for you as a young man. It is expected for you to be sexually active as much as you want, which is such a trap for you. It TAKES the strength and self-control of the Lord within to be willing to wait for the appointed time to awaken love.

But if you will trust God's plan, God's path, God's timing, you will enjoy all He has for you in the beauty you desire to pursue.

I want to leave you with something that Pat, who is just a few years out of college, wants to share with you:

> I am not perfect, so when asked to give advice in this book, I struggled with the thought of being hypocritical. The best advice I can give is to never count yourself out. I believe God can use anyone at any time to fulfill His plans. No one except Christ will ever be perfect, and this will hold true for as long as we live. I have struggled with many obstacles, especially sinful ones, and I still do. What helps to keep my mind focused is that even when you fall off the horse, you can always get back on. I use this mentality in my everyday life. There are many people in the bible and throughout history that really hit home with me, one of them being St. Peter. Peter was a lowly man but through God he was able to achieve great things. Peter, was a common fisherman who dropped everything to become a follower of Christ. He was also the first to come to Jesus's defense, but in the darkest hour, he denied Christ not once, not twice, but three times. The list goes on of unexpected people like St. Peter that were used in amazing ways and even some that did the most regretful things imaginable but God uses all types of people to fulfill His plan.
>
> You will be faced with more than three opportunities in your life to deny Christ and to choose the wrong path. You will also struggle more than three times. However, when you are confronted with these moments that test your character, take a second and choose the most honorable option. This will ensure that no matter the outcome, you can rest easy knowing you stood up for someone, reached a hand out to a fallen comrade, treated someone with respect even when it wasn't the easy thing to do and, at times, be the warrior you need to be. Just like Peter, you won't always choose the best option but try to focus the next time and of course get back on the horse.
>
> Pat

If you get off the path God has set for you, as Pat said, get back on the horse. God never counts you out!

IT'S YOUR TURN

Take the time to think about these questions from Chapter One. Your answers will help you in making clear and wise decisions for yourself. Don't skip this. This is your life. Take the time to make the changes in this area of sexual integrity.

JOURNAL: CHAPTER ONE

What do you want to receive from this study? What do you want God to show you the most about yourself?

Do you trust God has a good plan for your life? In what ways? And how?

Explain your understanding that marriage is a gift from God.

How can you avoid the voice of deception in your mind that tells you to reach out and grab the lie, as Eve did in the garden, to "see, taste, and eat."

Pick two of the five Scriptures from the ones listed in Chapter One, Making God's Case through His Word, and write them down. Explain why the verses are significant to you personally.

_____

_____

_____

_____

_____

_____

_____

TAKE ACTION:

Do you think it is possible to abstain from sexual activity before you get married? Why? Why not?

_____

_____

_____

_____

_____

_____

What is God's purpose in creating sex?

Does Mark's suggestion of the "5-second decision" make sense to you? How?

After reading this chapter, what 3 things can you put into action right away to strengthen your walk in the Lord with this subject of sexual integrity.

CHAPTER 2

IT'S YOUR CHOICE

Therefore be careful how you walk, not as unwise men but as wise,
making the most of your time, because the days are evil. So then do
not be foolish, but understand what the will of the Lord is.
—Ephesians 5:15–17 (NASB)

Let's take a walk. There is so much to cover. This place you are at right now is a very unique time in your life. From now through many years out of high school, your peers, friends, and girls will be pretty much a top priority to you. You need to be at a place where you choose these friendships and whom you are going to date wisely. It's your choice. No one is policing you. It's your own choice. I challenge you to be wise.

There are so many good things ahead of you regarding relationships, but if you don't have standards, goals, your identity as a young warrior, and the truth of God's Word deep within your heart, you will fall for everything and anything.

You absolutely do not want to be naïve and immature in this area at this time in your life. This is not the time to compromise your life. Friendships can accomplish a lot for you in this season, and one good friend can make a huge difference in your life. But one bad friend can do the same thing. The Bible says in 1 Corinthians 15:33 (NASB) that *"bad company corrupts good morals."* How will you choose?

I CHALLENGE YOU TO BE WISE.

MAKING CHOICES CAN BE VERY DIFFICULT

Every area we address in this chapter will concern choices that have to be made individually. Some are tough choices where you may need to end a friendship or a relationship with a girl that you know

is not God's best for you. There will be choices to make once you set standards and try sticking to them. A choice may come when you see the progressive actions of "how far is too far" and the importance of where you draw the line.

Whatever the situation may be, all of these choices come with consequences. If you make good choices, you will reap good and positive consequences. If you make bad choices, you will reap bad and negative consequences. The ball is in your court. You are being challenged to have high standards, and that comes with a cost. Please take *seriously* the choices you are making in your life. As you read this chapter and start to make some decisions for yourself, I trust that you will let the Lord show you His goals and His strategy for your life at this time. It is healthy to have many friendships in high school, especially including those of the opposite sex. He will show you how to choose wisely if you will only ask Him.

FRIENDSHIPS

We can agree; friendships are very important at this time in your life. Many times you'll find yourself going along with the crowd because you want to be a part of a group. Though it is a normal thing to do, often that is not a wise thing to do. When we want so badly to fit in, we sometimes do things we never would have been a part of had it not been this desire to belong to a group. Everyone wants to feel like they belong to people who care.

Before we go any further, I want you to hear from Matthew. His honesty will challenge and help you in this area of friendships and your self-worth. He is a father of two young boys. Listen up:

Let's be honest, guys. You will make mistakes. You will make bad decisions and that's okay. I've made a lot of mistakes along the way. I still make mistakes every day, but that's how we learn who we are, we learn our limitations and more importantly we learn what we are able to change from. That's how we begin to grow.

A lot of the mistakes that I've made when I was your age involved the friends that I chose to hang out with, the decisions that I made under peer pressure, the need to prove that I was just as cool or careless as my friends and the fact that I was unaware of my limitations.

Be aware of your limitations. Take a step back and ask yourself, can I be myself around these guys or am I acting the way I think they want me to be, how I want them to see me? Would I make these decisions if I was alone, if these guys weren't around?

Be honest with yourself. Respect yourself. Respect your peers, especially respect the females that you surround yourself with. Test yourself. Set personal goals. You may not achieve all of them, but at least you know what you are capable of, and you can find out what your limits are and what may be holding you back from becoming the man you want to be. Be aware of your temptations. Ask yourself, what's holding me back from being who I know I can be? Be aware of what behaviors need to be changed to improve and take action to make that change. Grow.

Guys, don't be overwhelmed by all of the expectations that surround you. You know what those expectations are. Don't feel like you have to prove your self- worth to your siblings, peers, friends, friends of friends, girlfriends, teachers, coaches, etc. Just be yourself. All the rest will fall into place.

It's taken me years to realize my true self. It comes with time. Life is a journey of growth. Now, as a father and husband, I realize that I don't have to prove myself to anyone. My self-worth isn't imprisoned in the car that I drive or the house that we live in or the lucrative dream job. My self-worth is coming to the realization of my limitations through honest true self-reflection. The realization of what I can create and the impact I can make on people that I come in contact with. The realization that I still make mistakes and the understanding that by God's grace I am forgiven and I am still able to learn and to grow each and every day.

Every single time I look at my two young sons, I see the same thing over and over again. I see hope. It's as clear as day. Simple, brilliant, magnificent hope. And I know that they will make mistakes along the way just like I did, just like you will too, but they will live and learn and grow into men. Just like you will.

Matthew

I wanted you to see this and take note. By Matthew's comments looking back, he saw what his friendships did for him in high school and the effect they had on his life. I hope you read it again and again because he is honest that one of his mistakes in high school was the friends he chose. He is challenging you to choose wisely. Look at this part again, "Take a step back and ask yourself, can I be myself around these guys or am I acting the way I think they want me to be, how I want them to see me? Would I make these decisions if I was alone, if these guys weren't around?" Answer these questions for yourselves. Be honest with yourself. It will help you. Matthew specified that we make a lot of mistakes in our lives and those mistakes help us to grow if we let them. I agree. I trust you will use all that he said to help you make wise decisions for yourself. "Be aware of your limitations."

"BE AWARE OF YOUR LIMITATIONS."

First Samuel 18 tells the story of David and Jonathan. They had a very close male friendship where they had each other's back. Even though King Saul was out to kill David, Jonathan stood by his side and had his back no matter the attack his father, King Saul, was planning for David. David and Jonathan's relationship had honor and integrity, respect and brotherhood.

It's good to have strong and healthy relationships. Friendships with guys and girls that bring out the best in you , are good for you, hold you accountable to what you are doing, who love to joke around and have fun. Someone who can be trusted with confidential information you share and who is not ashamed of the gospel of Jesus Christ.

There is nothing greater in the world, no greater treasure than to have friends you can trust and rely on. Choose your friends wisely. They can make or break your future.

A friend loves at all times.   —Proverbs 17:17

It takes time to search these people out. As a young man, these friends you make in high school can easily be a part of your life all of your life. What a great thought...choose wisely!

BULLYING

I have to address this topic of bullying because it is so out of control throughout every school in the country. To think that someone would purposely treat their peers in a way that steals every aspect of their heart, emotions, and spirit. It reeks with lies and destruction, and can last a lifetime in the heart and mind of the victim. To be made fun of or ridiculed takes the sails out of the victim's heart. They turn inward as isolation, rejection and hating themselves sets in. This is an awful way to be treated and one that MUST STOP.

Let's look at the dictionaries definition of bullying – "the use of force, threat, or coercion to abuse, intimidate or aggressively dominate others. Includes verbal harassment or threat; physical assault; emotional and cyber assault."

THE HEART OF A BULLY IS A COWARD

What makes someone a bully... someone willing to hurt another person to the degree that it shatters that person's heart and spirit? How is someone so angry within that they get pleasure in treating other's with such disdain? Or what is going on in the heart of a bully when they can laugh and make fun of someone to the point of causing such pain? THE HEART OF A BULLY IS A COWARD...someone that has to belittle others to feel good about themselves. If you challenge a bully, you will see them cower because, according to Webster's dictionary, a coward is "a person who lacks courage in facing difficulty, opposition; a timid or easily intimated person." Look at that; they are the ones who are easily intimidated, yet they make others feel like they have the authority and power over them. A bully speaks and acts from the darkness of their own heart.

Look at this Scripture...so much truth here:

There are six things which the LORD hates, seven that are detestable to him: haughty eyes, a lying tongue, hands that shed innocent blood, a heart that devises wicked schemes, feet that are quick to rush into evil, a false witness who pours out lies and a man who stirs up dissension among brothers. —Proverbs 6:16-19

It's imperative that we pull this apart:

First of all, it says that these are the things the Lord hates...hates! That's a strong word. In other words, the Lord detests these things listed. And look how they all can relate to bullying...

+ **Haughty eyes** – someone who is scornfully arrogant, who thinks they can say whatever they want and not care how it hurts you.

+ **A lying tongue** – most bullies lie about the person they are trying to harm. It makes them feel good about themselves. This is where they pick on the person constantly, day after day, spilling lie after lie, making it sound like the truth.

+ **Hands that shed innocent blood** – I know this is tough to put in here about a bully, but look how many teens have taken their own lives because of the bullying they had to go through in school. Just today, as I am writing, a 13 year old boy from New York was so profusely bullied he took his own life. Those who brought him to the place of such despair, where he took his own life, that is evil through and through.

+ **A heart that devises wicked schemes** – a bully usually knows exactly what they are doing to someone and very easily plans to make that person's life miserable. It's their plan to make fun and to be mean to you. That person is intentional in their heart to cause you pain. It's not about you; it shows you right away who and what that person is like on the inside. (*"There is deceit in the hearts of those who plot evil..."* (Proverbs 12:20a)

+ **Feet that are quick to rush into evil** – when someone is being bullied, others usually chime in and gang up on the person being bullied. It's usually not just one person doing the bullying. There is evil in a heart that finds pleasure in destroying someone else's life.

+ **A false witness who pours out lies** – a bully will say false things about their victim, threatening to harm them, yell in their face, make them feel like they are worthless. They are a false witness of the truth of who that person is. They say things that destroy the valued person you are...and it is very difficult when someone says, "just don't listen to them." It is very hard not to believe what is being said to you on a daily basis that is unkind and negative. It is NOT the truth. "*The Lord detests lying lips...*" (Proverbs 12:22a)

✦ **One who stirs up dissension among brothers** – …It says there were six things the Lord hates, but then says, no seven. Look at this last one…someone who spreads strife among brothers—strife means: bitter sometimes violent conflict or dissension. And this Scripture says among brothers. Your Christian peers that cause and bring anger, lies, manipulation, torment, gossip, threats, hate, is spreading strife among brothers.

As I said in the beginning of this segment…God hates what is happening with bullying…He hates what it is doing across the country in schools…GUYS, He hates it!

Please understand that if you are being bullied, it is NOT about you. It is about the ugliness and hatefulness in the other person's heart. I am convinced that a bully is someone who hates something within themselves or something going on within their home, and then they are causing so much torment to those they are trying to destroy because they hate who they are. Or they get such a kick out of controlling someone and causing so much hurt in that person. Their heart is cold and mean. That says so much more about them than it does about you. Again, it's not about you. They are cowards and know most people will not fight back or stand up against them. It is the ugliness of their heart…NOT yours.

PLEASE UNDERSTAND THAT IF YOU ARE BEING BULLIED, IT IS NOT ABOUT YOU.

If you are being bullied, you MUST do one thing for sure…You MUST tell your parents and the school. They need to know, and they need to get involved in what is happening to you on a daily basis. You cannot be afraid or intimidated going to school every day. That is no way to live. You have an inner courage in Christ that will help you through this. I know how hard it is, but you cannot let that person or persons steal your joy or your life. They count on you being afraid of them and feeling too sick to your stomach to go to school. (*"The Lord is close to the brokenhearted and saves those who are crushed in spirit...*" Psalm 34:18) He is near. He sees all of this. He will see to it that those who are causing you such pain will be chastised for their behavior. He will. He is your defender. He will help you heal from this. Tell someone and know it is not about YOU.

Let's talk a minute about suicide. Suicide is not the answer. To not live out the days the Lord has ordained for you here on earth because of someone's own ugly heart is not the answer for this. Suicide is never the option. I hope that the Scripture I pulled apart above will help you realize it's the other person's problem and not yours. They are being used by the enemy of your soul to drive you to this place of despair. I know it can feel unbearable. I know the loneliness it can bring...(*"a crushed spirit dries up the bones."* Proverbs 17:22b). I know how it tears you up as a person, but it is not the truth. Oh how I wish I had known that at your age. It. Is. Not. The. Truth. The truth is that you have your whole life ahead of you and, with the strength of your family and the Lord, you will get through this time. Suicide steals all that you were called to do for the kingdom of God. It is never the answer. It is not from God. There is a whole life ahead of you.

To the bullies reading this...and I know you are out there. Your heart is hard. To get pleasure out of controlling someone in this manner is exactly what the Lord hates. Think of it...if you, as a believer, are bullying your peers, He hates what you are doing. This is not just about the person you are tormenting, it is about you offending the Lord in treating someone in such ugliness. Do you understand? That person you are bullying is not the problem...your heart is. You need help. And that help only comes through Christ. I am not being super spiritual here. I am telling you the truth. Look within...what is going on? Why are you treating people in this way? What has happened to your heart?

> *What comes out of a person is what makes him "unclean." For from within, out of men's heart, come evil thoughts.* —Mark 7:20-23

You need to understand that because bullying is getting so out of hand in the schools, more and more states are trying to get laws on the books to press charges against the bully. I, and many others, are in complete agreement with that. That says something very strong. This is an ugly way to treat others. And a bully should be held accountable and responsible for the torment they are causing others. It is what a terrorist does. They torment. I trust that is not the way you want to learn your lesson.

Again, and from the Scripture above, treating people this way is coming from the hidden person of the heart. What is in a man's heart comes out of his mouth. *"For out of the overflow of his heart his mouth speaks"* (Luke 6:45). So the bully is being fooled by his own heart. Change your heart if you are that bully. If you are desensitized by others being so hurt by your actions, that is showing you what is going on within your heart. What you are doing is what the Lord hates. This is not who the Lord called you to be at all. He sees you so much more valuable to His kingdom and to others. I pray you get help for your sake. Again, I pray you reach out to a youth pastor or a pastor that you will be honest with, and who can help you get free from the brokenness in your own heart that is causing damage to others. And I pray that when you receive His love and forgiveness, you will genuinely go to those you have hurt and ask for forgiveness. They need that too.

WHAT IS IN A MAN'S HEART COMES OUT OF HIS MOUTH.

FRIENDS WITH BENEFITS AND SEXTING

I hate having to address all of these issues. But it is what your generation is dealing with, and I am not afraid to talk about it or tell you the truth. It's just a bummer this is how perverted this one topic of sex has become in our society. And you got caught in having to deal with it.

The sensitive subjects that I must address is the concept and choice of "friends with benefits" and "sexting."

Friends with benefits are two friends of the opposite sex who are having sexual relationships, mostly oral sex, with each other with no commitment and, supposedly, no emotional attachment.

This is dumbfounding. This cheapens you and the girl. I'm sorry if that sounds harsh, but it's the truth. I want to know who in the world decided that this was an acceptable form of relationship with a friend of the opposite sex. Sex with no attachment? Hold on...that is not truth. That might be what you think is happening... BUT you are actually joining yourself with someone emotionally, physically and spiritually. It is an intimate sexual act. So many guys are caught in this. You could easily be one of them. Because God made sex to be such an intimate act between a husband and wife—a commitment of the hearts, the spirits, and the emotions—it would be pretty foolish to think that this kind of casual sex won't affect you.

SEX WITH NO ATTACHMENT?
HOLD ON...THAT IS NOT TRUTH.

You have been programmed as a young man that this is just being a guy and it's fulfilling a need. I'm sorry, but it goes against the man God is calling you to be. When you learn to treat girls in this casual way, how will you find the one the Lord has planned for you? He never intended for you to use girls for your own gratification and then walk away looking for another one. I just want you to know truth and walk in it. Read in the book of Proverbs 7—a story of a young man lacking judgement. He went with what was going to feel good. He was warned, but went anyway. In the end, he paid a great price. The Lord wants to raise you to become a man who will fight against the tide of the culture. Someone He can count on... someone He can mold and pull aside to bring strength and dignity back to this culture. Can He trust you to stand on this battle field with Him and be a light and voice for your generation in this area?

THINK AGAIN

Let's think this through one more time. It is unwise and immature for you to think that this kind of lifestyle is helpful to you. I have had numerous girls crying to me because they lost a great guy friend when they became involved in "friends with benefits" and now the guy no longer wants anything to do with them. To bring sex in any form into a friendship with a girl not only ruins that friendship, but it degrades, dishonors, and disregards both people involved and completely severs the trust and confidence that a friendship is supposed to give.

Understand that this is such a deterioration of not only you as a young man, but of your worth, your identity, your character, your future marriage, and definitely your relationship with the Lord.

If you need to talk to someone, please find a Christian counselor, a teacher/mentor/Youth Pastor you can confide in and get yourself free and clean from not only the sin of this but of the mindset.

I spoke at a Christian school years ago to all the guys for a chapel. I gave them the opportunity individually, with the principal's permission, to come and talk to me after if they had any questions or wanted prayer. I didn't know it at the time, but the most popular guy in the school wanted to talk. The principal gave us the teacher's room to talk. This senior, good looking, fun, athletic, most popular guy in the school, confided in me on how he uses girls for "friends with benefits." He had been feeling convicted by it and finally admitted what he was doing was wrong. We talked for an hour. With tears in his eyes, he repented and asked the Lord to forgive him. I trust when you realize what this choice is truly doing to you, like this young man, you will repent and walk away from this mindset and the way to treat a girl for your own sexual needs.

Remember, your choices will follow you. Dating is supposed to be fun. If you choose to date God's way, you will enjoy yourself. Will you be tempted? Yes. You are challenged in a day and age where anything and everything goes. You must think outside of that box, and enjoy the journey the Lord has mapped out for you. That means you will walk a narrow and different road. Not without challenge, but with strength in your heart.

WHAT'S UP WITH SEXTING?

The subject of sexting is a major problem in many, many high schools. It is, right now, the number one topic I am asked to speak on along with bullying. First, may I say that I have no idea where this started and why it has become acceptable behavior among so many teens. This rests on both guys and girls. The girls are just as involved in this as the guys.

When asking a girl to send you a naked picture of herself, you are immediately participating in child pornography if she is under the age of 18! And it is plain and simple pornography if she is older! Most of the time when a girl sends a picture to a guy he is not the only one who looks at it; it is usually sent to many of his friends. This kind of activity will morally spin out of control. More than anything, it is blatantly open sin for those involved. Some girls have told me they feel pressured to send pictures of themselves. I can't make this any clearer than to warn you that sexting is looking at and promoting pornography. The girls have no clue what that does to you as a young man and how images stay in your mind. I'm trying to get you to see your responsibility in this. Sexting is a form of pornography. It is out to lead you to so much more than you bargained for. Sexting also is a degrading way to treat a girl. How is this honoring her? How is this respecting her?

SEXTING IS LOOKING AT AND PROMOTING PORNOGRAPHY.

These two Scriptures immediately come to mind. Again, you want the truth. You do not want to continue doing things that becomes a lifestyle of destruction for you.

These are Jesus' words:

You have heard that it was said, "Do not commit adultery." But I tell you that anyone who looks at a woman lustfully has already committed adultery with her in her heart.

—Matthew 5:27-28

You are the salt of the earth. But if the salt loses its saltiness, how can it be made salty again? It is no longer good for anything, except to be thrown out and trampled by men.   —Matthew 5:13

These words are to make us all mindful of the truth of the Word of God. Do you see in the first Scripture that it is committing adultery to look at a woman/girl the way sexting is being used. Think of that, in the heart of God, it is committing adultery in your hearts. No one is talking about that truth or even saying it from the pulpit. Just because it isn't talked about doesn't nullify the truth that it is committing the act of adultery in your heart. It was never God's plan for any of you as young men. It is pornography. Again, sexting is pornography. Think about that…what is wrong with that thought? Do you see the addiction that can come from sexting? **Addiction stalks you.** Do you see how a girl's body can become just an object to you?

ADDICTION STALKS YOU.

Listen to what Mike has to say about pornography:

This is truly a sickness that I still battle with. As a teenager, I happened on a large collection of magazines. It has been a constant fight ever since. I will say only by God's grace this can be beaten. It truly is a slow fade that can control your thoughts.

Mike

It is not just magazines for your generation; it is your phone which is with you 24/7! Mike is being honest that he still battles with something that started as a teenager. Take this seriously. We will talk more about pornography in the next chapter.

Let's look at this second Scripture. It is very powerful because we are called as the salt of the earth, but look what it says: *"if the salt loses its saltiness…."* We all use salt on food. It makes it so much better. BUT this is saying we can become tasteless, no longer good for anything when we choose to go against the will of God. Understand that God sees your life ahead of you; He knows the effect this will have on you in the very near future. It is a choice—it is a choice to walk in integrity and character, and it is a choice to be involved in this sort of extreme indulgence in bodily pleasures and especially sexual pleasures. It's a "5-second decision."

Sexting has become so serious that there are some states considering legislation that those who send and those who receive sexting would be issued a criminal charge of child pornography. This is a serious matter in so many ways. Not only criminally but it steals you away emotionally, physically, spiritually and mentally. It makes you exploit girls, and to see their bodies as just objects instead of someone to be valued, loved, protected and cared for. If you are deeply involved in sexting, you need to get help. Stop the onslaught. Confess and repent to the Lord and to those who may have been used and tainted in this. There is forgiveness in Jesus. The slate can be washed clean. Go to Him to set you free.

IT IS A CHOICE TO WALK IN INTEGRITY AND CHARACTER.

LOOK ONE MORE TIME

In wrapping up this segment, there is a lot to think about and many choices to make. These were all topics that are surrounding you on a daily basis. You want to be a young man who is wise, who can make wise decisions with the friends you choose to walk through the halls of your school with. Walking with integrity and honor to stop the bullies and stand with those who are being bullied. To not be afraid to stand up for what is right among your peers. I know that is so hard to do and is very challenging, but you are called to be that voice that rescues those who are hurting. You can pray for them under your breath if that makes you feel more comfortable at first. Then get your footing and begin to be that voice and outstretched hand to that comrade next to his friend.

Friends with benefits and sexting cannot have a place in your life. They are destroying the man within. As you begin to honor and treat girls with respect, you will see many of your friends follow. I truly pray you take these topics seriously and realize they have no place in your life with your friends who are girls. It cheapens both of you and robs you of having great friend-ships. And it steals the blessings and peace that God wants to give you freely. He is trusting you to give this over to Him and let Him change your mind-set and cleanse your heart.

You are called to be a world changer. Put yourself above the pack. Decide to be the fish that swims in the opposite direction from the tide. You can choose the wide road, which many are on. Or you can choose the narrow road where only a few are called. The choice is up to you... CHOOSE WISELY.

Enter through the narrow gate; for the gate is wide and the way is broad that leads to destruction, and there are many who enter through it. For the gate is small and the way is narrow that leads to life, and there are few who find it. —Matthew 7:13-14 (NASB)

IT'S YOUR TURN

Take the time to think about these questions from Chapter Two. Your answers will help you in making clear and wise decisions for yourself. Don't skip this. This is your life. Take the time to make the changes in this area of sexual integrity.

JOURNAL: CHAPTER TWO

Have you ever had to make a tough choice in your life? What was it and how did you handle it?

Your choices will follow you – after reading Matthews comments, what kind of choices can you make in friendships that will strengthen or change who you are currently hanging out with now?

Do you have at this time girls as friends in your life? If so, do you see the importance of valuing that relationship? In what ways?

_____

_____

_____

_____

_____

_____

Are you willing to stand up for those who are being bullied around you? If so, how?

_____

_____

_____

_____

_____

_____

If you know someone who is a bully, how will you now approach this to stop what they are doing?

_____

_____

_____

_____

_____

_____

TAKE ACTION:

How are you going to change your mind-set regarding sexting?

Do you now understand that sexting is really a form of pornography? What does that mean to you?

Do you realize what "friends with benefits" is doing to you and the girl you are involved with?

If you are involved with "friends with benefits," how can you change? Who can you talk to?

If you are going to be this warrior, man of honor and integrity, then what kind of action will you take in treating a girl you plan to date with respect and dignity?

RAISING THE STANDARD

How can a young man keep his way pure?
By living according to your word.
—Psalm 119:9

Dating is a very involved subject and one that needs a lot of attention and wisdom. It's about being ready to honor and respect the girl you are interested in. Not to treat her as one of the guys or someone to take advantage of or use. The statistics are very high that early dating leads to early sex.

Temptation is something everyone deals with in dating. To date differently from the world, what would that even look like? God has one standard, the culture has no standard. This chapter will help you discover how to set standards and boundaries, the strength of self-control, the importance of drawing the line on "how far is too far" and what to do with all of the sexual temptation that comes to you in a dating relationship. Let's get started.

GOD HAS ONE STANDARD, THE CULTURE HAS NO STANDARD.

I say this from years of working with teens, you shouldn't date until you are 16 years old, and even then you should double date or group date until you are 18 years old. Ok, I just heard you laugh! As much as that sounds old-fashioned to you, this is the best way to enjoy the company of the opposite sex. This holds you accountable to yourself, her, both of your parents and the Lord. There is no pressure to have sex. It is a safe place to truly get to know her and for her to get to know you. I hate to burst your bubble, but most of the girls you date in high school will not be your mate for life. Putting so much emphasis on that dating relationship can cause so much unnecessary pain. That is why it is good to group date a lot and not just be alone with each other all the time. That makes for a healthier relationship all the way around.

This is Jon's comments to you about dating during high school. He is very honest with you. Listen to his heart on this matter:

Dating. Love. Sex is all part of this world, but if not kept in check, it can be very harmful and will impact not only your present, but your future as well. It is very easy to get sucked into the dating game in high school and even justify it is ok because the person is a Christian. But temptation during this time frame is extremely high. Peer pressure and even just flat out curiosity can get the better of you. Holding hands turns to kissing which turns into touching which turns into kissing the body which turns into sex very quickly. The Bible reminds us in 1 Corinthians 6:18-20... *"Flee from sexual immorality. Every other sin a person commits is outside the body, but the sexually immoral person sins against his own body. Or do you not know that your body is a temple of the Holy Spirit within you, whom you have from God? You are not your own, for you were bought with a price. So glorify God in your body."*

Are you open enough as a young man to have a Christian mentor or another adult in your life with whom you HAVE to share your dating details? If not, you are not ready to date. Accountability, TRUE accountability, is a must for any godly dating relationship. Being truly accountable will help you stay clean. God wants us to be holy. (See 1 Thessalonians 4:3.) It is God's will that you should be sanctified: that you should avoid sexual immorality.

Jon

I like how Jon was driving the point home to have someone who holds you accountable in your dating years. It is very important that you have that "go to" adult who you can be honest with at any given time. Today's society puts so much pressure on young people. From TV to movies to music, they all present the same thing: "What is wrong with you if you are not going out or having sex with someone...you're 15 years old?" "What are you waiting for?" If you don't handle this pressure to date in a healthy manner now, it can set a negative precedent for all your dating years. It is so imperative that you don't rush into dating relationships if you aren't willing to give it the attention and wisdom it needs.

I understand you have the pressure of asking girls out. Yes, I say pressure because it sets you up for a possible rejection that can be very hard to take. Even though rejection could be scary, don't go with today's culture by using social media posts instead of calling a girl or asking her out face to face.

I challenge you that chivalry is not dead! You may not be familiar with that word. Chivalry means – gallantry, courtesy and honor, the noble qualities a knight was supposed to have. Do the gentlemanly thing...you ask her out; and do not wait till she asks you and don't use social media. Girls want to know you are interested in getting to know them. Most girls love to have doors opened for them. They still love to get flowers. Don't let anyone fool you, girls love those small things; it lets them know you care and are interested. How you date will follow you into your marriage. It matters what you do and how you treat that girl now. Make wise choices raising the standard.

CHIVALRY IS NOT DEAD!

HOW ARE YOU PREPARING

There are healthy and good reasons to be dating. A few of them are listed below. Read through them, and then we'll talk further!

- To help build friendships with the opposite sex
- For healthy, mature personal and social development
- For choosing a marriage partner
- For having good, clean fun
- To help encourage the other person's relationship with Jesus Christ

Society and the media have absolutely warped the whole concept of dating. I know that at this time in your life you may not be thinking about dating someone for marriage purposes. But you must understand that your choices for dating now will follow you into your marriage.

God is wise. He has a plan. You must have high standards, without compromise, and great moral convictions before you ever decide to date.

Believe me, I have watched so many girls and guys make crazy mistakes just because they *had* to have a boyfriend or girlfriend.

Remember, it was while Adam was sleeping that Eve arrived. God knows what He is doing even in these young dating years you are going through. I know that you want to enjoy this time, and you should! It's important that you have a plan and standards ahead of time before you go out.

God's got this. Enjoy this season and time of your life. Make good, clean choices for yourself. This means don't embrace the media's idea of dating. Your definition of dating needs to come from the Word. "Don't arouse or awaken love until it pleases" (Song of Solomon 2:7). Be wise... You will never regret it.

GOD'S GOT THIS.

RAISING STANDARDS AND SETTING GOALS IN DATING

It is important to do what is right instead of what is popular. This should matter to you.

WHAT IS A STANDARD AND WHY IS IT IMPORTANT?

A standard means to take a strong and aggressively-held position on a matter...to put together boundaries that you will not cross or break so that you can keep your walk strong before the Lord, yourself, your family, and friends. Setting a standard, therefore, means you take the time to write out responsible actions you will allow/not allow in a dating situation.

You *must* have the boundaries set and the line drawn from biblical truths long **before** you go out on a date.

WHY IS IT IMPORTANT TO HAVE STANDARDS?

You want the girl to know where you stand regarding what you will allow in the relationship.

When you haven't thought about standards/boundaries before you go out on a date, you will open yourself up to so many compromising situations it will make your head spin. You will have to make decisions at times in the spur of the moment. That's why if you already have quality goals, boundaries and standards set ahead of time, you will be better equipped to make wise and responsible decisions on matters that you were not expecting or able to handle.

Below are a few important standards in dating. Hopefully, this will help you understand.

PHYSICALLY

What <u>you</u> allow to happen will be the line that is drawn. You must have these standards firmly set if you don't want to fall to sexual sin. Answer these questions honestly for yourself. The more you get to know the girl you are dating and the longer you go out, you will need to add much more to this list.

+ What is the meaning of a kiss?
+ What about kissing on the first date?
+ What will your response be when she says no to your roaming hands?

ACCOUNTABILITY

It is so good to have someone, preferably a mentor or youth pastor, that you can trust and who will hold you to the boundaries and standards you set. Being accountable to someone keeps you honest in your dating relationships.

+ Discuss your standards with your date up front on the <u>first</u> date, so there are no questions about where you stand. She will feel secure in knowing you are taking the lead in this.
+ Avoid being alone as a couple.
+ Be accountable to someone else (a friend or mentor).

SPIRITUALLY

You can have a blast in dating because you will be so free in knowing that you belong to Him and that He wants the best for you. You would be accountable to the One who started all this from the beginning. This makes for a very healthy and fun dating experience.

+ Date only Christians who have the same convictions as you.

+ Pray together before the date asking the Lord to keep your hearts pure and your relationship with Him front and center.

+ Ask God for help in choosing wisely whom you will date.

MEDIA

The cultural media—and this includes so many movie and rap stars—are so reckless about portraying relationships. They have no boundaries and, therefore, they set no boundaries. If you live your life by their way of thinking, and their promotion of sex, you will fall for things you never thought you would. Understand guys the principles of the Lord are not in any of their movies or rap video's. They are drawing you away from His standards and His value of women.

If you follow the media's standards, you will lose such a sense of moral right and wrong that your heart will be far removed from the heart of God. You will be shocked at how fast this will happen if you believe the media over the integrity of God's Word.

+ Don't put yourself in front of a movie together at home in hers or your game room lying on the couch; it leads to compromising situations very quickly.

+ Remember, people in movies and TV aren't really in love or having a relationship. All you are watching are two people acting out fantasy. Realize that any arousal you may feel while watching this with the opposite sex, may lead you both down a path you never intended to walk.

+ The media is out for ratings and to make a lot of money! They are very aware that sex sells. Don't fall into the greed and lust of their pleasure. Do you see the importance of setting standards and having boundaries? It will change the way you date, making it healthier.

Look at the standard and advice Mike wants to share with you regarding dating:

My advice on dating in high school would be to make sure that whoever you ask out, she loves the Lord first and foremost. As a hormonal teenager, it is so easy to give in to temptation and do what the world says is natural and expected. I had God's favor in having a very godly girlfriend in high school. It was truly by God's grace that He put my girlfriend in my path. The temptations were very real, but both being believers, kept me on the straight and narrow.

Mike

Mike admits the temptations were very real; he is being honest with you. However, he and his girlfriend set their boundaries and standards first, helping them to stand strong when they needed to.

THE TEMPTATIONS WERE VERY REAL

I want to share with you another testimony this time from a former female student. She has a great story of the standards she had before she got married. It's good to hear this from a female's perspective, someone who has walked what we are trying to convey here.

Tammy has been an officer in the United States Navy for over 10 years. Guys, she flew double bladed helicopters! Being a female in an environment with so many men, Tammy needed to be very sure of who she was as a woman of God and what she wanted in a man she would marry. She related to me a story that happened to her early in her career.

Tammy was asked out to dinner by a guy she was beginning to date. At dinner that night, she was very upfront with him and told him that she would not sleep with him at any time in the relationship. That she was saving herself for marriage and wanted him to know right off the bat where she stood with that issue. After a bit of time, he excused himself to go to the restroom and never returned to the table. He left her at the restaurant. She had to call a friend to come and get her. Of course, she cried over the situation and was hurt. But she was not going to compromise her heart to anyone until she made it to the altar. Tammy could have easily gone with the world system: sleep with whomever you date. But she chose another kingdom. Tammy is married now with two children. Her decision did not keep her from her heart's desire.

I want to add something very important here...the guy she was out with that night was a coward. I say that because the right thing to do on his part was to tell Tammy he wanted sex to be a part of their relationship, so this was not going to work between them. Enjoy her company for the rest of the evening, finish dinner, and take her home. Instead, he left her there, forcing her to call a friend to come and get her. It says so much about him and his lack of manhood. I believe he was 25 years old at the time. Obviously, that is not how to treat a girl, that is not being a man of character. Set those standards and boundaries for yourselves.

TEMPTATION

Let's talk about temptation before we continue on.

Temptation falls upon all of us. It's what we do with that temptation that directs our actions. All temptation begins in the mind. If you choose to dwell on that temptation, you are more apt to fall to the desire of it. Your mind...what you think about and temptation go hand in hand. The more you **"allow"** your mind to dwell on anything you'd really like to do, the more likely you are to do it.

> *Watch and pray so that you will not fall into temptation. The spirit is willing, but the flesh is weak.* —Matthew 26:41

To be curious and think about sex is normal, but to be obsessed with that curiosity or thinking is lust. Lust is a continual commitment of the mind. A continual commitment is one that will not let go of an image or of a desire. This is where pornography grabs a hold of someone so quickly. Someone once said, "The world says you are free in sex through indulgence." God says, "you are free in sex through control." Until you can control this area of your life and your mind, you are not free. Here are three areas to think about:

Temptation is NOT sin. *Jesus was "tempted in every way...yet did not sin"* (Hebrews 4:15). Temptation is a thought. It does not have to lead into sin. You have a choice of what you will do with that thought. If you dwell on it, it will grow. If you let it go, it will have no effect. Jesus used the Word when He was tempted in the wilderness. That is your defensive weapon as well. It would be great to use the "5-second decision" here, recognize the temptation and immediately ask the Lord to help you. If you get used to using this tactic, you will be able to face temptation more victoriously. This may take time, but give it a try. It is temptation that is luring you in to sin.

TEMPTATION IS NOT SIN.

Keep yourself out of compromising situations. Your game room, alone with a girl, in the dark, watching a video, playing video games, lying on the couch, is a very strong compromising situation. This can lead to many sexual encounters that were never intended or planned. Don't set yourself up. This Scripture should help you to see where this is coming from.

> *When tempted, no one should say, "God is tempting me." For God cannot be tempted by evil, nor does he tempt anyone; but each one is tempted when, by his own evil desire, he is dragged away and enticed. Then, after desire has conceived, it gives birth to sin; and sin, when it is full-grown, gives birth to death.* —James 1:13-15

Look how it says that each person when they are carried away and enticed by their own lust, this is when temptation is formed. Understand where temptation is coming from…

Satan uses temptation to make us fall. Satan, the very enemy of your soul, so desperately wants to entice you away from God's plan and purpose for your life. Recognize his tactics. He is not very creative; he will use the same thing over and over until you catch on to his scheme. His plan is to knock you down and keep you there. Satan's ultimate fight is with God, and he goes after us, God's kids, to get to God and to entice us to fall. God is not tempting you…remember, it's coming from the enemy of your soul.

I want you to read a word of encouragement that Jonathan wrote on the area of temptation. The character, trust, priorities, and commitment needed in a relationship to combat temptation. Pay attention…it comes with a challenge.

> Here is the thing I've discovered…being a man is all about character. The best relationships, the best marriages, even the best friendships are always based on trust. No one can logically or emotionally refute that with any level of credibility. Even people who aren't living a godly life will tell you that if they can't trust their relationships, then they will end that relationship. Our character is what builds trust with others and that trust is the foundation, the life line, of every relationship.
>
> When you think about it, this life is all about relationships, no matter if we are talking about our relations with others or with God. In the end, when we die, we spend eternity with the people around us, which is why our relationships with others is so vital. Our problem in every relationship, the things that can ruin every connection we have, are the choices we as men make when faced with temptations. This means if we want strong relationships then it's only logical for us to have a strong character, and our character is formed by the priorities we choose.
>
> Priorities are the decisions we make before we are faced with temptation. When it comes to temptation, unless we decide who we want to be, we will give into the emotions or feelings of any given situation and live a life void of integrity and truth. Our priorities are what will keep us clean when temptation comes our way. Let's face it, if you don't decide before a date with your girlfriend on how you will handle a situation that may get a little too involved physically, you won't be able to do the right thing and make a wise decision on the spur of the moment. That temptation can be progressively overwhelming.
>
> The men who are responsible with this God given gift of sex are the ones who decided 'before' to commit to what they want and

should do. Let me let you in on a secret, while some women may be distracted by great abs or rock solid pecs, the best women in the world find character, trust, integrity and right priorities to be the sexiest thing on the planet. These women are the ones that will change through life with you, no matter what.

So decide today, right now, what are my priorities? What will I devote myself to? Then, once your priorities are made, once your commitments are firm, your decisions become easy and you will be able to avoid and overcome overwhelming temptations.

Jonathan

Decisions and priorities come "before" you go out on that date. Jonathan brings it home to you to realize temptation can be overwhelming many times, especially on a date with your girlfriend. If you have priorities set up first, it can help you make wise decisions when temptation tries to come along.

DECISIONS AND PRIORITIES COME "BEFORE" YOU GO OUT ON THAT DATE.

STAND UP UNDER SEXUAL TEMPTATION

No temptation has seized you except what is common to man. And God is faithful; he will not let you be tempted beyond what you can bear. But when you are tempted, he will also provide a way out so that you can stand up under it. —1 Corinthians 10:13

This Scripture says, *when* you are tempted, not *if*. Therefore, it is inevitable that you will be tempted. Paul is saying here that there is a way to stand up under it. So, how do you stand up under temptation?

Here are just a few things to think about:

<u>Run/Flee</u> – Do not stick around to see how strong you are or are not. Do not think you can stay under the emotional and physical force and handle it. Your flesh will want to be fed…you need to flee when temptation is overwhelming. Remember, there is always a way of escape.

<u>Accept Responsibility For Your Choices</u> – Our own behavior is always our responsibility. Do not allow your friends' choices make your choices for you. You must take responsibility for what you know is right when temptation comes. We all are tempted by different circumstances, situations and things. What triggers that temptation for you? It will be personal to you. When you recognize what that is, make the choice needed to walk away.

<u>Be Accountable</u> – Question your own conduct – Why am I dwelling on this? Am I spending time alone with God and His Word (this is key)? What am I watching or listening to? Friends get in each other's faces! (*"As iron sharpens iron, so one man sharpens another"* Proverbs 27:17.)

These are just a few things to help you out with this battle of temptation. Be aware, temptation lurks all around us. You will have temptation all of your life. It's what you do with the temptation that will direct your heart and spirit. What a great opportunity for you to learn how to recognize and respond in a different manner than you have been used to regarding temptation. You won't be perfect at it…none of us are. But when you can recognize it at your age and place it before the Lord quickly, you will be very far ahead of the game and will be able to teach others the same.

Let's keep moving on…there is so much more to learn…

SELF-CONTROL

Self-control is not for those who are weak…it is for the strong and committed. It is possessing power, having good sense, self-denial, self-sacrifice. It is a discipline not many want to practice. The message screaming at you so loudly from the mass media is that it is unrealistic to ask you to control your sexual appetite. That it is unrealistic and foolish for you to believe in self-control over self-indulgence. What a deadly trap that assumption is to many of you. God is not out to rob you of something. He is out to bless you and give you something of value and price.

In His extravagant love for you, God has designed the most beautiful way to express intimate love between a man and a woman here on earth. To be a slave to that pleasure outside of marriage is the world's view of sex. Their view defiles sex, making it impure, selfish, and indulgent. It causes you to be a slave to your desires and not a master of them. Therefore, you lose control.

Despite what the culture says, self-control—not self-indulgence—frees you from being held captive by your desires. Christian teens have been deceived and bought into the lie that they don't need to control their desires for sex but to indulge them. You are told, "You're just being a kid", or "Who cares, it's no big deal", or "What's wrong with you? It's a natural thing, what are you waiting for?"

IT TAKES COURAGE TO MAKE A STAND

Self-control is a commitment to yourself, your future wife, and to God that you will not satisfy your desire for sexual activity until the proper time.

Intimacy is knowing and loving someone very deeply. It is total life-sharing. It is the joy of being fully known.

What you are being fed in our culture is instant gratification (just the physical) over intimacy and purity of heart. Remember, we said sex isn't just physical; it's emotional, mental, and spiritual. When you engage in sex outside of marriage (and that includes oral sex), with every partner you are with, you lower the significance of sex with your future spouse.

Intimacy and getting to know someone so fully can only come with time, commitment, faithfulness, friendship, respect and unconditional love.

The Word of God specifies that when a man and woman come together in a sexual relationship, *"they will become one flesh"* (Genesis 2:24). You become one with that person not just physically but emotionally, mentally, and spiritually.

I have watched many students have a very hard time breaking up with their girlfriend and not understanding why. Or they would always seem to run back to that person. Why? Could it simply be because they felt the bond of being one with each other?

God wants your sexual experience to be what He intended it to be. He knows the reasons why He placed the boundaries. They were completely and lovingly for your good and your ultimate pleasure.

Remember, it was God who noticed that Adam was alone: *"It is not good for the man to be alone. I will make a helper suitable for him"* (Genesis 2:18). Adam didn't ask, God had noticed. He noticed Adam could use a companion. He wanted man and woman to walk together, share their hearts, share sexual pleasure, have children, enjoy each other's companionship, comfort each other through the ups and downs of life, and love the Lord their God with all their heart, mind, soul and strength. He calls it very good, and He knows one of the best ways it can be obtained is through denying yourself for the sake of another.

PRACTICE SELF-CONTROL

Here is an analogy in practicing self-control. I am a huge college football fan. Think about these athletes who are serious about excelling in their chosen sport. They are disciplined and self-controlled when they want to compete and excel at a level that will give them their greatest victory, gratification and satisfaction.

They can't sit around eating fast food and chocolate, drinking coke or pepsi, barely practicing, and then expect to compete at the level they want! They must practice self-control, self-denial, and self-sacrifice.

YOU MUST PRACTICE SELF-CONTROL

The same is true when you are practicing self-control with relationships. You can't sit around watching TV, movies and listening to sensual music that have so much sexual content in them and then expect to keep yourself pure in thought and action. It simply doesn't work that way. As you are looking to stand strong in a reckless world, you **must** practice self-control, self-denial and self-sacrifice.

> *Everyone who competes in the games goes into strict training. They do it to get a crown that will not last; but we do it to get a crown that will last forever. Therefore I do not run like a man running aimlessly; I do not fight like a man beating the air. No, I beat my body and make it my slave so that after I have preached to others, I myself will not be disqualified for the prize.* —1 Corinthians 9:25-27

Challenge yourself in this goal of self-control. Without self-control you have no defenses. Don't make flesh decisions on who you are right now. Make decisions on who you want to be 10 years from now. There is a whole life ahead of you. I said from the beginning of this book, you are in a battle. And that battle is between the flesh and the spirit. Who is going to win? To walk in the spirit and not be controlled by the flesh, will change everything about the way you live. Look at what Galatians 5:16-17 says:

> *So I say, live by the Spirit, and you will not gratify the desires of the sinful nature. For the sinful nature desires what is contrary to the Spirit, and the Spirit what is contrary to the sinful nature. They are in conflict with each other, so that you do not do what you want.* —Galatians 5:16-17

You are empowered by the Holy Spirit to rise up and fight this battle. God is for you, my friend. He is waging this war alongside of you, you are not fighting alone. He is wants His purpose for your life to win out in the spirit and not in the flesh! This battle will be your whole life.

HOW FAR IS TOO FAR?

> *It is God's will that you should be sanctified: that you should avoid sexual immorality; that each of you should learn to control his own body in a way that is holy and honorable, not in passionate lust like the heathen, who do not know God; and that in this matter no one should wrong his brother or take advantage of him.* —1 Thessalonians 4:3-6

Obviously, this is a very hot topic. Everywhere I have gone to speak, this is the number one question I am asked: *How far is too far?*

It has always been curious to me how teenagers, really people in general, always push things to the edge; wanting to see how close they can go to something before it is called sin. When you think in that manner, you are not mature enough to date yet. Living that kind of lifestyle will have big downfalls sooner or later.

ONE FIRST TIME

There is only **one first time** in having sex. It should never be a game to you.

The question really shouldn't be, "How far is too far?" The appropriate question is, "How can I get to know this person in a better way personally, and how can we build our relationship together in Christ and in serving others?"

You have a lifetime with your married partner to fulfill the sexual desires that God has placed within each of you. To push arousal to a place of wondering when to stop defies the very purpose of what God intended from the beginning.

Do not be so concerned about how far is too far, rather be concerned with how you can be wise, set apart, have integrity and character, a leader in a reckless world.

He who trusts in himself is a fool, but he who walks in wisdom is kept safe. —Proverbs 28:26

LOOK DEEPER

Let's see if we can get you to understand a little more about this subject.

When something no longer satisfies, we always want more. That's how most people get addicted to drugs, alcohol, and pornography. Regarding sex, there is a progressive action that takes place as well. When you do one thing for a certain amount of time, it eventually won't be enough; you will want more. The chart below will show you what I mean:

Holding hands → hugging → kissing → prolonged kissing → touching private areas with clothing on → heavy touching of private areas with some clothes off → sexual intercourse

Look at the progressive action that is taking place. Holding hands is the start of a physical relationship, and then the progression begins.

The problem with many in your generation today is that they seem to go from holding hands to oral sex in just a few dates. Somehow, they seem to think that this is ok and that the line is drawn somewhere with that. I did not put oral sex on this chart because so many teens are confused by that sexual act. We will talk about it later.

I'd like to add here that when you jump from holding hands to a sexual act so quickly, it is only lust. You can try to justify it…thinking that it's love in just a few dates, but in actuality it is just lust. You miss out on a friendship being built between the two of you. You are pushing for something that has consequences and trying to justify it as ok. In the process, you are ruining what could have been a great relationship with someone.

THINK ABOUT IT

One way to know that you have gone "too far" is if you create a desire in someone that you cannot fulfill and still be pleasing to God.

You have to understand that if a man arouses a woman with a desire to have sex, he is defrauding her (in other words, taking advantage of her, as we just read in the opening Scripture of this segment). He has violated her because he is not her husband, and he cannot satisfy those desires within the boundaries God has set up. *If you both want to keep your relationship pure and within God's plan, you need to talk to each other.* You do not want to draw out physical desires that will cause the other person to stumble.

Realize that guys are aroused by sight, and girls are aroused by touch. Once your hormones have been aroused, you begin to limit your freedom to make wise and clear choices. This is why it is imperative to have already made up your heart and mind about your standards and where the line is drawn—and stick with it!

You have also gone too far when you cannot make sensible and responsible decisions and act on them immediately. Making out prepares the body for sexual intercourse and causes your feelings and emotions to overpower your mind and cloud your decisions.

REALIZE THAT GUYS ARE AROUSED BY SIGHT

These are just a few ways to help you recognize the buttons you have pushed that can easily lead you over the edge in this area. Because sex is such a powerful desire, it is foolish to think that you can go so far and then stop.

Your flesh doesn't know or care that you are only 14 years old or so, or that you want to live a righteous life. All the flesh knows is that it wants to be fed, so however you feed it, it will always want, and sometimes demand, more.

DRAW THE LINE

In drawing the line on how far is too far, the line is to be drawn right after the kiss, and no further. Again, one thing leads to another. When you can't righteously satisfy the physical desires building up in that girl you are with, you are headed down a slippery slope to fornication.

As I said above, you have a lifetime with your married partner to enjoy the pleasures of intimacy. Outside of marriage, you will only cheapen it and cause it to be of less value for both of you.

> *"Everything is permissible for me"—but not everything is beneficial. "Everything is permissible for me"—but I will not be mastered by anything. …The body is not meant for sexual immorality, but for the Lord, and the Lord for the body. …Do you not know that your body is a temple of the Holy Spirit, who is in you, whom you have received from God? You are not your own; you were bought at a price. Therefore honor God with your body.* —1 Corinthians 6:12-13, 19, 20

LOOK ONE MORE TIME

Take a breath—that was a lot of info! But I trust it was very thorough and will give you many tools in raising the standard regarding dating. There is a lot to think about and put into practice. You want to make wise decisions long before you are placed in a compromising situation. It is wise to be prepared instead of caught off guard. It is good to have fun and to enjoy your dating experience. It is supposed to be fun to date—yet the world has placed so much pressure on you to do it their way, that it has trickled into the Christian world and caused so many young people to compromise their values and walk with the Lord.

As you begin to implement the things that were written in this chapter and challenge yourself to date in a manner that will respect and honor you and the young lady you are dating, you will see how much more you can relax and enjoy the relationship with her. How much fun it can be to get to know someone without having so much pressure put on both of you!

God is fun! He wants you to enjoy your relationships. Try it His way and raise His standard high…you will be pleasantly surprised!

I will instruct you and teach you in the way you should go; I will counsel you and watch over you.   —Psalm 32:8

RAISING THE STANDARD 79

IT'S YOUR TURN

Take the time to think about these questions from Chapter Three. Your answers will help you in making clear and wise decisions for yourself. Don't skip this. This is your life. Take the time to make the changes in this area of sexual integrity.

JOURNAL: CHAPTER THREE

With all of the information in this chapter on dating, do you think it is realistic to date in this manner? Give reasons how.

Give 3 ways you can prepare your heart going out on a date.

While so many of your peers are living recklessly with relationships, how are you going to be different?

_____

_____

_____

_____

_____

_____

What are your priorities in dating? What will you devote yourself to?

_____

_____

_____

_____

_____

_____

_____

Self-control not self-indulgence frees you. Explain.

_____

_____

_____

_____

_____

_____

_____

TAKE ACTION:

What triggers sexual temptation for you?

Once you recognize those triggers, what plan do you have to combat them?

What part does TV, movies, computer games, music videos, and music play in your life? What impact has it made on you?

Give 5 ways you want to treat the girl you date with respect and dignity.

After reading the segment in this chapter about "how far is too far", what is your opinion on where you draw the line and what boundaries/standards will you put in place to keep from crossing that line?

You are challenged in this chapter with the fact that God sets one standard and the culture has no standard. Explain what that means to you and how you can raise the standard in your own life with this topic of dating.

_____

_____

_____

_____

_____

_____

_____

_____

THE SELLING OF SEDUCTION

Do not conform any longer to the pattern of this world, but be transformed by the renewing of your mind.
—Romans 12:2

There is a huge battle going on for your attention. I've said that a few times in this book so far. The world is calling after you, and the kingdom of God is calling after you. They are in complete contrast to one another, and they are at war with one another. The one you give the most attention to, the one you allow to speak to you the most, will be the one you follow.

I will probably step on a lot of toes in this section of the study, but I'm not looking to sugar-coat anything. I have no desire to be politically correct. There is too much at stake for you at this time in your life to not be honest with you. It is my desire to tell you the truth. There is much to say, so let's get started.

TURN ON THE LIGHTS

The entertainment industry reflects the culture we live in. There is an onslaught of distorted images and ideas of how we are to live our social lives. Daily exposure to this kind of message will affect the way you think and the way you will respond to life decisions.

When we use the term "the world," we are referring to the system of the world—what that system believes, its behaviors, and its way of thinking—that is completely opposed to the Word of God and, of course, the kingdom of God.

Please understand, there are two voices crying out for your attention. Once you become de-sensitized to the deception in the world system, the kingdom of God will seem old-fashioned and non-relevant to you, with all of its moral values simply to be disregarded. Before you even realize it, the world has so completely influenced your heart and disguised the truth of God's Word with a lie that you end up looking like the world even while you are saying that you are still a child of God. It's time we change that. It's time to take back the kingdom of God in your life.

> *Do not love the world or anything in the world. If anyone loves the world, the love of the Father is not in him. For everything in the world—the cravings of sinful man, the lust of his eyes and the boasting of what he has and does—comes not from the Father but from the world. The world and its desires pass away, but the man who does the will of God lives forever.* —1 John 2:15-17

The media (which consists of TV, movies, internet, music, e-mail, facebook, snapchat, youtube, texting, twitter, Instagram, books, magazines, advertising commercials, cable news, newspapers, etc.) is today's means of communicating with others. If you can't or don't recognize the counterfeit that lies in a lot of these, you will fall desperately into the world's system.

What much of the media is doing today is giving you false values, a false sense of love, and a false sense of security. Gentlemen, don't be fooled. The majority of what you see and hear is a direct attack on you as a young man.

WHAT HAS ENTANGLED YOUR MIND?

Listen closely to this… I am going to shed **light** on something that you have heard before but maybe not in this way. Do you realize the best way to ruin your life; your heart, your emotions, your spirit, your friendships, your personality, your relationships with the opposite sex etc., is through your mind using pornography? It is vital that you take this seriously. You are at war and you need to see it that way. What eating disorders do to girls/women is what pornography does to boys/men…it's a monster within. It completely devalues the very person God has created you to be.

The pornography industry, through so much of the entertainment industry, is a multi-billion dollar business. Read that again…**a multi-billion dollar business**. The industry is banking on you getting addicted at a young age (beginning at 10 or 12 years old) so that they have your heart, mind, soul and money the rest of your days. It is designed by the enemy of your soul to drag you into such deep darkness—to keep you from being the man you are called to be by God. It causes shame, guilt, condemnation, darkness of the soul. It keeps you from being able to look at a girl in a pure manner. This perversion does not care what color skin you are, how old you are, if you are a Christian or not…it ruins marriages, finances, ministries, families, careers…it likes to hide deep within your soul…it has no boundaries. It entices boys/men who at any time for any reason open themselves up to this.

While I was a high school teacher, I specifically remember two boys came to me crying because they were so addicted to pornography they had no idea what to do. Both came to me separately in private. Both were seniors. One was black and one was white (I say that because it knows no color). Both were amazing athletes. Both loved the Lord and wanted to serve Him. But both were entangled, twisted in their hearts and minds at 17 years old because of this one monster that was ruining their lives. I know they were not the only ones dealing with this, but they were the ones who came forward. After speaking to them at length, giving them Scriptures to memorize over their minds, praying for them, I had them both go to speak to a pastor I recommended. But understand, I would never have known unless they told me. It was hidden. It was a secret. They were suffering in silence. That is what sin does…it makes you hide out of fear and shame. There is a very well- known quote that speaks volumes…"we're as sick as our secrets."

"WE'RE AS SICK AS OUR SECRETS."

Remember in the garden when Adam and Eve ate from the tree they were told not to eat from? What was their first response when the Lord was looking for them…."We were afraid so we hid ourselves because we were naked." Look at that—fear, hiding, shame…three of the most powerful tools the enemy uses over sin in our lives. In the case of pornography… those three things will put you in a battle for your very lives. Shame is the greatest enemy of the heart. It helps to keep you hiding for fear that others will find you out. Do you see where sexting can also open the door to so much of this? My friend, the Lord has a better way…He wants things in the light. For the Lord knows that once things are in the light and once you expose those things hidden, they can no longer have a hold on you. He is fighting with you in this. *He is for you.* When light is shed in darkness, we are set free!

> *Your eye is the lamp of your body. When your eyes are healthy, your whole body also is full of light. But when they are unhealthy, your body also is full of darkness. See to it, then, that the light within you is not darkness.* —Luke 11:34-35

Pornography is a counterfeit to the real thing! The definition of counterfeit: *made in exact imitation of something valuable or important with the intention to deceive or defraud; pretend; unreal.* Wow!…look at that. You are being lied to, deceived and carried away by something that is not real and cannot satisfy. It is a counterfeit of the real thing; it is intended to deceive you. Please take a minute and read that again. The counterfeit's goal is to deceive you. It's to make you think that what you are looking at or doing while you are looking at these pictures/video's will satisfy. It is a counterfeit and will keep you from true intimacy with the woman God has for you. It's producing lust in you, not love. Lust has a job, a purpose and an assignment to lure you away from the will of God in your life in this area of sexual integrity. You create a habit and that habit creates you. It wages war against your soul. It produces distance instead of closeness. It robs you of true intimacy. It is a deep darkness within. It is a counterfeit to the real thing. Pornography is a sin that robs God of His glory in the gift of sex and sexual integrity.

PORNOGRAPHY IS A COUNTERFEIT TO THE REAL THING!

Look at it this way, if the enemy wanted to keep you from serving the Lord and bringing many to His kingdom, wouldn't it make sense to go after the very thing that would entangle you and keep you from affecting lives for the kingdom and from receiving all that God has promised you as a man? What the world paints is a false sense of the true worth of a woman. It exploits her, makes her only an object. It is a counterfeit to the real thing. It paints a fantasy in your mind that no one can live up to. All of a sudden, you will find yourself in an addiction you can no longer control. I said it before and it is true, addiction is a stalker. It would be the best destructive plan the enemy of your soul could offer your mind and imagination to destroy you as a man after God's own heart.

Unless you go after this with a vengeance, it will control you all of your life. A pastor friend of mine shared with me when I asked him about this problem of pornography. He was adamant that he knows no one who has struggled with this who got free alone. He said that it is imperative that you find someone to hold you accountable to your thoughts and actions. It is not a battle you can handle alone! He also said that "if you are the only one that knows your secrets, you are an accident waiting to happen." That is so good and so true. At the end of this chapter, I will have some Scriptures you can begin to memorize and get into your spirit. BUT, you must take the action of shining a light on this addiction in your life no matter how embarrassed you are or afraid to admit what is going on. Do not let yourself, your friends or your enemy convince you that you are ok and that you can handle this alone or that it's ok your just a guy and this is normal. That is a lie. You **must find** a pastor, an older man in your life you trust, a friend who will hold you accountable to your thoughts and actions. This is a battle between flesh and spirit. You have a whole life ahead of you, please get out of hiding and find your freedom—it awaits you.

STOP! THINK FOR A MINUTE...

I am asking you to stop at this point and grab a piece of paper. Be really honest with yourself. What are you basing your life and relationships on? Think about these questions and answer them honestly for yourself (no one is looking), then answer the questions below:

+ If you are looking at pornography, are you willing to tell someone you trust for help?

+ If you are sexually active, why?

+ Do you base your value on girls by their appearance or who they are from the heart?

+ Would you be willing to sacrifice your Christian walk just to fit in to the world system? Or should I ask, have you sacrificed your Christian walk and are you fitting into the world's system right now?

I am only asking you these questions because you may not be asking them for yourself. This whole area of pornography doesn't just go away when you get married. I am trying to give you information and a way to get help so that years into your marriage you don't find yourself losing your wife and family because of this one addiction. I am around families right now that have been destroyed because of the addiction to pornography that the husband was involved in since he was your age and hid it and never got help. This is not a game. This is real life.

THIS IS NOT A GAME.

After you have answered the questions above, you may need to make a game plan on how to change your way of thinking. What are you watching and who are you wanting to impress? What I am saying is that your life cannot consist of what the world's value system says is right. Those in the world's system have no intention to honor God in any of their decisions. They do whatever feels good, or seems right to them, being held accountable to no one, especially the Lord. Let that sink in a while.

I want you to read what Loren says here. This is a great word that fits this area perfectly.

> Truth. Quite possibly, the most controversial word in today's culture. Why? Simply because it is, by definition, narrow. In light of that fact, the truth can be offensive, no matter how much you don't want it to be. Jesus said that He is the Way, the TRUTH and the life, and that no man comes to the Father but by Him. Now that is a very hard statement, because it immediately requires you to make a decision. It's either Jesus's way or no way.
>
> So what does the Bible, compared to today's culture, have to say about your struggles? Culture would have us think that what we feel is right, as long as we are not "harming" another person. This has been presented as a defense for things like fornication and pornography. People may say things like: "it's private" or "that's my personal choice." What's the problem with that? Well, according to the Bible, it's wrong. Period. Now here we have two views which are directly opposed to one another. If the Bible is true, we have to deny how we feel, no matter how strongly we feel it, and this can be extremely difficult!

In steps the warrior. It is absolutely impossible to live in this world, as a Bible believing Christian, and not be offensive. Your very life will convict people around you, and they will malign you because of that. Your secret struggles matter, because God knows them all and requires us to be holy. For example, pornography is something I struggled with for years. I thought that it was OK because I wasn't actually going out and having sex with a lot of women. But this lifestyle is very deceiving. With pornography you have a tendency to stop looking at a girl/woman in the way that God sees them. That leaves you with the liberty to define them how you want; a liberty that does not belong to you. For me, after I had my daughter, God illuminated to me this flawed mindset and used that to turn my heart. Now she is a constant reminder that each woman is a child of God that God loves much more than I'm even capable of loving my daughter.

My encouragement to you is to not fall for the lies that the culture puts out there. Just because it's shiny, doesn't mean it's clean. Everything that looks good doesn't necessarily smell good. Even when it hurts, stand up for what you know is right and true, and we know that is the Bible.

Loren

This is so good. Your secret struggles matter to the Lord. God is not angry with you; He knows you are living in a fallen world. He is not willing to leave you there in that place—He is willing to help you in and through this. You realize a few of these guys that are writing to advise and encourage you are letting you know the struggle they have/had with pornography? You are not alone in this. Take the time to find someone to talk to through this. Hold yourself accountable to someone you trust.

WHO WILL YOU BE GIVING AN ACCOUNT TO?

We cannot trust the entertainment industry. They are after the almighty buck. They do not care who gets hurt by what they are letting you absorb through your eyes. Think of it in this way: when your life on earth is over, you won't be standing before the world giving an account for your life. You *will* be standing, however, before the King of Kings and Lord of Lords to give an account.

No matter how popular and seemingly free in spirit these celebrities, whether entertainers or athletes, live their lives, they also will bow their knee one day before the only King of Kings and Lord of Lords. The Bible declares that *every* knee will bow and *every* tongue will confess that Jesus is Lord. So this tells us that every celebrity; entertainer; athlete; talk-show host; writer, producer, and director of TV, movies and videos; singer; songwriter; and dancer will all one day bow their knee before Jesus. So I ask you again, are you willing to sacrifice your true relationship with the Lord for the world's system?

Look at where you are in your life right now. You are serving one kingdom or another. Which one are you serving? Which one has your undivided attention?

> It is written: "As surely as I live, says the Lord, every knee will bow before me; every tongue will confess to God." So then, each of us will give an account of himself to God.   —Romans 14:11-12

COME OUT OF THE DARK

We have allowed the world system to infiltrate the church. The lust of the flesh, the lust of the eyes, and the pride of life!

We're beginning to see no difference between the world and the church. Teens are just as sexually active in the church as they are in the world. You are taking your cues from another kingdom. And you have been duped. It all sounds good, and the media tries to make it all look good, but you are being seduced by a world disguising itself as freedom. It's time to come out of the dark and go after the temptation that is before you on a daily minute by minute basis.

SEDUCTION: A FALSE PROMISE

The world system is all about seduction and lust, trying to convince you that your passions are to be indulged rather than controlled. The words *seduction* or *seduce* according to Webster's dictionary means "to persuade to disobedience or disloyalty; to lead astray usually by persuasion or false promises." Seduction is dressed up to do one thing, to flatter you and then trap you. The seduction I am talking about is the one coming from the world's view of sex outside of marriage.

Do you notice how often you are being seduced when you turn on the TV? How about when you are at the movies? Start paying attention to what you are watching with your eyes: what you see, read, and take in through your eyes will greatly affect your view of the quality of sexual fulfillment. Your eyes are like a camera – taking pictures that stay in your mind to deceive you into thinking that you are missing out on something or need to indulge in whatever your feelings are saying.

Look at the romances portrayed on TV and in the movies. Not much friendship or relationship occurs. Within 1-2 days, they supposedly are madly in love with each other and involved in a sexual relationship. Teenagers see this and act it out – expecting the same instant gratification. You have just been seduced into thinking it is love when all it has been is lust disguised as love through seduction. The greatest seduction is that the media makes it all look so very enticing!

This is how they seduce girls/women. Look how many soap operas there are on TV. They are no longer just on in the afternoons; there are plenty on in the evenings. They are meant to make women dissatisfied with their boyfriend or husband in hopes that there is a McDreamy somewhere in their path. They lie to the girls as much as they do to you as a young man.

LUST DISGUISED AS LOVE THROUGH SEDUCTION.

TAKE NOTICE

All of this seduction is based on a false promise of forbidden love with no consequences. It's a way of cheapening sex and worse cheapening love.

So often so many TV shows, movies, and music are wrapped in the spoils of seduction. Once sex is presented with no boundaries like this, the door is opened to all kinds of perversion. When God tells you to abstain from all of this behavior, it's an act of His love for you. He is not *trapping* you in anyway. He is *protecting* you in every way.

When you lust after things—having an intense desire for something—it begins to rage a war within your soul. The world system says that sex is used to gratify lust and desire. There is no love, no commitment, and no responsibility involved. When you fall to the seduction of the world system, it begins to choke the life of God's truth and His Word right out of you.

THE DEATH SQUEEZE

Take a minute to imagine a python snake. A python doesn't poison its victims like the rattler or cobra. Instead, the python squeezes the breath out of its victims. What I see happening to so many Christian teens is just like the death squeeze of the python. As you begin to compromise your morals and give in to the world's system of casual sex, the world system, like that python snake, begins to slowly wrap its mindset and behavior around you and choke the very truth of God's Word and nature out of you.

First, you are deceived and then slowly but surely you begin dying spiritually and emotionally. I always wondered why so many seniors, after they graduated from Christian high schools, were seduced into the world system within the first three months of their college experience. Something was out to squeeze the breath of truth out of them, and, unfortunately, it didn't take long to succeed.

The world system is powerful and alluring, but it can only get the upper hand on you if you are not bathed in the truth of God's kingdom and His Word. Every student I have spoken to that has returned to the Lord after being persuaded by the world's system has said the same thing, "It cost me more than I thought I would have to pay." The seduction of the world's system is a counterfeit to the very thing you are longing for: true love.

DISLOYAL

Lust and selfishness are designed to lure you out of the will of God. When you reduce love to lust, it blinds you to the worth of others and the glory of God. It will corrupt your life. It will lead you into disobedience and disloyalty.

Remember that part of the definition of seduction is disloyalty. Disloyal to whom or to what? Disloyal to God, yourself, your friends, your family, your future wife and kids and the ministry God has planned for you. That's exactly what the enemy is hoping it will do to you so that you won't fulfill the very destiny God has in mind.

Once you fall for this, and you begin to become desensitized, you end up having no desire to do the things of God in your life. Your worship will stop, your desire for youth group will stop, you will become bored at church, and you will no longer spend time alone with the Lord. So you see, when you stand alongside the world's system in the area of immorality, you will lose more of yourself than you ever imagined!

> *Don't let anyone look down on you because you are young, but set an example for the believers in speech, in life, in love, in faith, and in purity.* —1 Timothy 4:12

ACTION

It is time to step up!

I know this is a lot of in-your-face truth. But it desperately needs to be said so you understand what you are up against and can find and live in freedom. As you recognize the contrast between the world and the Word, you are going to need to take clear action and make crucial decisions. Not easy but possible. Your future depends on it.

In taking action, you must begin to let go of areas in your life where the world's system has more authority over your life than the Word does. That is always difficult to do, but you will never be able to move on to what God has designed for you unless you let go of what is holding you back.

WORK IT OUT

You are about to go through training. You have to re-train your mind, your way of seeing things, hearing things, thinking things, and saying things. When you start to train **your eyes** toward a pure heart, you will start to notice that what the world offers is cheap. When you start to train

your ears toward a pure heart, you will start to notice that what the world offers is foolish. When you start to train **your mind** with the Word of God, you will see that much of what the world offers is drenched in lies and deception.

When you go through training, it will require commitment, courage, and tenacity unlike anything you've done before. You will need to turn some things off, stop going to certain places and parties, choose different friends, and get involved in a good youth group. We are talking about re-training years of thinking for some of you. This will take time and commitment to accomplish. But I challenge and encourage you to take the action that is needed to be free from the pollution that the world has blown in your face.

It is for freedom that Christ has set us free. Stand firm, then, and do not let yourselves be burdened again by a yoke of slavery.
—Galatians 5:1

One of the best ways to go through training is with another friend who is looking to walk in the integrity of the kingdom instead of the world. Then you will be able to walk this out together. Setting goals and getting your eyes, ears and mind thinking truth over lies.

WE ARE TALKING ABOUT RE-TRAINING
YEARS OF THINKING

WHAT ARE SOME CONTRASTS?

Below are some examples of the contrast between what the world says and what the Word says.

When you allow lust, selfishness, and seduction to lure you in, you begin to think and act as the world does. The world's view suddenly becomes your view.

+ **The world says,** "Live together, marriage is old-fashioned, you don't need to get married."

♦ **God says,** *"Let marriage be held in honor among all and the marriage bed be undefiled…"* (Hebrews 13:4 NASB).

♦ **The world says,** "There is nothing wrong with being a homosexual or a lesbian, or marrying someone of the same sex."

♦ **God says,** *"Therefore God gave them over in the lusts of their hearts to impurity, that their bodies might be dishonored among them. For they exchanged the truth of God for a lie, and worshipped and served the creature rather than the Creator, who is blessed forever. For this reason God gave them over to degrading passions; for their women exchanged the natural function for that which is unnatural, and in the same way also the men abandoned the natural function of the woman and burned in their desire toward one another, men with men committing indecent acts and receiving in their own persons the due penalty of their error"* (Romans 1:24-27 NASB).

♦ **The world says,** "Abortion is ok, it's not a baby yet. Besides it's her right, her body, her choice."

♦ **God's Word says,** *"For you created my inmost being; you knit me together in my mother's womb. I praise You because I am fearfully and wonderfully made; Your works are wonderful, I know that full well. My frame was not hidden from You when I was made in the secret place. When I was woven together in the depths of the earth, Your eyes saw my unformed body. All the days ordained for me were written in Your book before one of them came to be"* (Psalm 139:13-17).

♦ **The world says,** "It's just sex; it's your hormones; you're young, enjoy yourself now; if it feels good, do it; you can't help yourself."

♦ **God says,** *"Do not be deceived, God is not mocked; whatever a man sows, that he shall also reap"* (Galatians 6:7 NASB).

Remember, you are preparing yourself as a man of God with integrity, character, and a solid understanding of His love for you. But while you are waiting for all that God has for you —I encourage you to not have one foot in the world and one foot in Christianity. You will be miserable.

This needs to be a clean, clear decision to put both feet in one of those worlds. This is your decision. No one can make it for you. I'm here to give you the tools to live with a clean heart, a victorious life in this reckless world. <u>But you have to *want* to.</u> No one can want this more for you than you do for yourself!

So I pose another question: what has the potential to lure you into a trap? What keeps knocking at your heart's door to lure you away to be disloyal to your Heavenly Father? No condemnation, it's a challenging thought. When you know that answer, your training will begin.

FIRST ACTION

Here are some tools/Scriptures I told you I would give you to memorize and get into your heart and spirit to combat what you may have put into your mind, heart and spirit regarding pornography. Now, anyone can memorize a Scripture—it's when you meditate on that Scripture that it will begin to affect your heart and to set you free. Remember, the Word of God is living and active and sharper than any two-edged sword. His Word is alive. You can trust it. Did you ever see a two-edged sword in action? (every super hero movie has them!) It cuts in every direction your wrist sends it. You are a warrior of the King—use your sword; your freedom is at hand...

Create in me a clean heart, O God, and renew a steadfast spirit within me. Do not cast me away from Your presence and do not take Your Holy Spirit from me. Restore to me the joy of Your salvation.
—Psalm 51:10-12

Therefore putting aside all filthiness and all that remains of wickedness, in humility receive the Word implanted, which is able to save your souls. —James 1:21

Therefore do not let sin reign in your mortal body so that you obey its lusts, and do not go on presenting the members of your body to sin as instruments of unrighteousness; but present yourselves to God as those alive from the dead, and your members as instruments of righteousness to God. For sin shall not be master over you, for you are not under law but under grace. —Romans 6:12-14

Commit yourself to the LORD; *let Him deliver you; let Him rescue you, because He delights in you.*   —Psalm 22:8

Come now, let us reason together", says the LORD. *"Though your sins are like scarlet they shall be as white as snow; though they are red as crimson, they shall be like wool.*   —Isaiah 1:18

Those who look to Him are radiant; their faces are never covered with shame.   —Psalm 34:5

You are already clean because of the word I have spoken to you. Remain in Me, and I will remain in you. No branch can bear fruit by itself; it must remain in the vine. Neither can you bear fruit unless you remain in Me.   —John 15:3-4

…When he saw Jesus, he fell with his face to the ground and begged him, "Lord, if you are willing, you can make me clean." Jesus reached out His hand and touched the man. "I am willing," He said. "Be clean!" And immediately the leprosy (bondage) left him.   —Luke 5:12b-13

This is a great start. I could have given you hundreds more. The Lord is for you. He loves you so much and wants you free from any bondage that is out to capture your mind and heart. Take these Scriptures and fight for yourself. Write them on 3x5 cards and give the time to let the Word work for you. It didn't take one day for you to get into bondage—it won't take one day to be free. It's like hitting a sledge hammer against a wall in your house. It won't dent it right away, but in time it will do much damage. Do damage to the enemy of your soul. You are worth it to everyone around you and worth it in your relationship to the Lord. He is fighting for you and with you.

DO DAMAGE TO THE ENEMY OF YOUR SOUL.

LOOK ONE MORE TIME

In wrapping up this segment on the selling of seduction, I want to encourage you in this battle. The fight for your attention rests on your choices and your will. This is a winnable war.

You might have to make one or a few of these choices...to turn off the TV, stop going to movies that are sexually enticing, stop listening to the music that draws you into sexual impurity, stop sitting for hours playing video games, begin walking away from friends who don't want to go where you are headed, let go of the girlfriend you know is not God's will for you. And the list can go on and on.

God loves you so much. He wants you to have the best that this life has to offer in relationship with the opposite sex. And His best is that you live in the boundaries He has set, not bowing to the views of the talk shows and media.

You have the responsibility to protect yourself from the world's view. Will this be a tough road? Absolutely. Is it an impossible road? Absolutely not. Remember, you are on the narrow road, but that road leads to life. So I challenge you to take the time and begin to ask the Lord's forgiveness if you have fallen into the traps of the world's view. Ask Him to help you sort through your current way of thinking and make some changes.

YOU ARE THE MOST INFLUENTIAL PLAYER
FOR YOUR GENERATION.

You don't want to put this off. God has invested so much in you already. There is too much He wants to do in and through your life at this young age. You have the potential to be a world changer! You can encourage those around you to live clean hearts and victorious lives. But you can't do that unless you have grasped these truths for yourself, and really begin to stand strong in a reckless world.

You will have the potential to bring many of your friends and peers along with you. Isn't that what it is all about anyway? Don't ever underestimate how the Lord can use you at this time in your life. As a child of the King, you are the most influential player for your generation. What a privilege. What an honor. A powerful warrior is in the making.

IT'S YOUR TURN

Take the time to think about these questions from Chapter Four. Your answers will help you in making clear and wise decisions for yourself. Don't skip this. This is your life. Take the time to make the changes in this area of sexual integrity.

JOURNAL: CHAPTER FOUR

The pornography industry is a multi-billion dollar business. It makes billions every year. What does that say to you? What does that show you about pornography?

If you are looking at pornography, are you willing to tell someone you trust for help?

Do you base your value on girls by their appearance or who they are from their heart and personality?

The quote from my pastor friend said, "If you are the only one that knows your secrets, you are an accident waiting to happen." What does that mean to you? Does that resonate with you and how?

TAKE ACTION:

Would you be willing to sacrifice your Christian walk just to fit into the world system? Or have you sacrificed your Christian walk to fit into the world system? Whatever your answer is...explain why?

So much of this chapter gave you Scriptures to memorize and get in your spirit to help you stand against the onslaught coming at you on a daily basis. Take two of those Scriptures and write them out here and explain why you chose those two to begin your fight for yourself.

What actions can you take in regards to the temptations that come at you on a daily basis?

What has the potential to lure you into a trap? What keeps knocking at your heart's door to lure you away from being disloyal in your heart to those in your life and to the Lord?

CHAPTER 5

THE WARRIOR WITHIN

Be strong and let us fight bravely for our people and the cities of our God. The LORD will do what is good in His sight.
—2 Samuel 10:12

I want to break this up a bit here and talk about how to become that Warrior Within and try to help you to understand what that means to you as a young man for your generation. You have an opportunity more than most other generations before you to be a voice of authority, reason, and truth. Not a voice of rebellion that some students your age have on the national news, but the voice that speaks life through strength of the truth. God's got your back...

To be a warrior in this day of social media where everyone scrutinizes every move you make, and people get offended at the smallest thing. You will need to be able to rise above the noise of the crowd and hear what the Lord is saying and how He wants to lead you to be His voice, His leader, His warrior for your generation. He has a purpose for you to fulfill in this earth that was picked individually for each of you. What does that mean and what does that look like? Let's read on...

Here is something Aaron wants to encourage you by...Aaron has a great word about your purpose and being a warrior - listen up...it's some good advice:

> So teach us to number our days, that we may apply our hearts
> unto wisdom.   —Psalms 90:12

When you look at a tombstone, most people notice the name, birthdate and date of death. But the most important part of the tombstone is the dash between the two numbers. In that little dash lies the story of your life. Your failures, struggles, temptations, trials, triumphs, victories and successes are all represented by a simple dash. With that said, I have a simple question. What are you doing with your dash? Most days it is a struggle to do the right thing. We are constantly faced with temptations and pressures from the world, our families and friends. These impediments can sometimes seem daunting and even insurmountable. Nevertheless, God has designed and equipped you to withstand it all and produce good fruit. Your purpose is calling you. Your purpose is counting on you to make the right decisions now, so that your fruit will be nutritious. As young people, we tend to get an uneasy feeling in our gut about the decisions we make or the company we keep. The next time you get that feeling I want you to remember these words, "your purpose is counting on you." It may not mean much to you today but making the right decision now saves your future self a ton of grief.

Sometimes the struggles are not necessarily external, but rather internal. Your greatest enemy can be your "inner me." There can be a level of uncertainty and anxiety that plagues you, causing you to succumb to the pressure. I would like to encourage you today. I have good news. The pressure is not meant to kill or even harm you. The pressure is there to strengthen you. When we go to the gym to lift weights, we add more weight in order to get stronger. That weight is simply more pressure. God does the same thing with us. He allows us to feel the pressure only that our faith and our spirit man can be stronger. You have value in the earth, and more importantly, you have value in heaven. God wants the warrior he designed within you to come to the forefront. Take your rightful place. Fulfill your God-given purpose. <u>Make sure your fruit is fit for the King</u>. How can God say well done if you refuse to do what you were designed to do? Your future will thank you for making the right choice today. Make your dash speak louder than the dates. God is listening for it.

Aaron

This is a very mature call from Aaron that encourages you to fulfill your God-given purpose—that your purpose is counting on you to make the right decisions now. That is so good. What a charge for you at this season in your life. What changes do you need to make? Read Aaron's words again and again. What a call to you as a warrior within!

The Lord has purposed you to be a man of valor (personal bravery) and integrity. It is a call to every young man who has made Jesus their Lord and Savior. I want to use a few stories from the Word of God to make this case of charging and challenging you to run after the things of God. If you choose to live out the warrior the Lord has placed within you, you will see a leader for your generation that will affect hundreds of young men and women for all eternity. Are you up for the challenge?

IN THAT LITTLE DASH LIES THE STORY OF YOUR LIFE.

HIS HEART

> *But the Lord said to Samuel, "Do not consider his appearance or his height, for I have rejected him. The Lord does not look at the things man looks at. Man looks at the outward appearance, but the Lord looks at the heart."* —1 Samuel 16:7

I know you are probably familiar with this story of David being anointed King of Israel, but let me point out a few things to help you see your journey through his story...

In reading this Scripture, the Lord is saying that your appearance, what you look like on the outside, whether you work out to build six pack abs or run marathon's to stay in shape, He is looking for the hidden man of the heart. What are you like with your friends and what you are like at home? How do you talk to adults and how do you talk to girls? What are you texting to your guy friends, what are you texting to girls? Do you show respect? Do you challenge yourself to embrace your role as a young man of integrity and character? Are you kind to the kid sitting by himself in the lunch room, not joining the crowd in bullying him just for the fun of it. Who are you as a hidden man of the heart?

When David was anointed King of Israel, he was just a young man of about 10-15 years of age. Long before he took the throne of Israel, God saw in him a young man, a young warrior who's heart was open to not only worship the Lord but to honor all the things of God. When Samuel came into the house he "thought" the oldest son was God's choice for king. Why? Because of his appearance....Samuel went down all seven sons of Jesse and the Lord kept telling him no, it's not him. When Samuel asked if there were any other sons, Jessie said "there is one more, the youngest" and called David in from tending the sheep. As soon as he walked in the door, the Lord told Samuel, "it is him." Understand how often others "think" it's the most popular athlete in the school, it's the most well-spoken student, it's the smartest student, it's the guy with the most friends, it's the guy with the greatest sense of humor, it's the guy who gets all the girls. Though all of those guys may be good guys, it's the heart that matters to God...it is not as other's "think" that leader should be.

God knows the thoughts and intentions of the heart. David was not perfect. We know his story. We know his sins and shortcomings. But that did not stop God from wanting and still using him as King. Why? His heart was always willing to repent and run back to the Lord. God can work with and through someone with a heart like David's.

THE WOUNDED HEART

As I have reiterated in this book, there is a war going on…it's a war that started the moment you received Jesus as your Lord and Savior. And what happens in war? You get shot at. Many of you reading this are dragging your heart with you. You are carrying wounds that have not healed and are still bleeding. I want to share something from an amazing book called *Wild at Heart* by John Eldridge. Let me quote a portion and then let's talk about it:

> Those blows you've taken—they were not random accidents at all. They hit dead center. Charles had a gift and calling to speak into the hearts of men and women. But his wound tempted him to be a loner, live far from his heart and from others. Craig's calling is to preach the gospel, like his father and great-grandfather. His wound was an attempt to take that out. He's a seagull. All he can do is "squawk." Reggie—His dad wounded him when he tried to excel in school. "You are so stupid, you'll never make it through college." He wanted to be a doctor, but he never followed his dream.
>
> On and on it goes. The wound is too well aimed and far too consistent to be accidental. It is an attempt to take you out, to cripple or destroy your strength and get you out of action. The wounds you've taken were leveled against you with stunning accuracy. Hopefully, you're getting the picture. Do you know why there's been such an assault? *The Enemy fears you. You are dangerous bigtime.* If you ever really got your heart back, lived from it with courage, you would be a huge problem to him. You would do a lot of damage…on the side of good. Remember how valiant and effective God has been in the history of the world? You are a stem of that victorious stalk. (*Wild at Heart*, 2001)

If you are reading this with a wounded heart, and it could have come from many different things, please understand that as a young man professing Jesus Christ as your Savior in this generation, you are considered a dangerous and major threat to the kingdom of darkness. And the only way to silence your voice and steal your strength is to weaken your heart to the point that you are no longer interested in the things of God or wanting to follow your purpose. Instead, you are content to sit at home after school, playing video games for hours and hours on end, and letting your heart die, merely just going through the motions of life. Don't let your wounded heart make you quit now...there is an answer....and that answer is Fight For It! Which means strengthen your spirit, emotions and mind in the Word of God. Fight against those words spoken over you that have stolen your voice and made you a chicken that squawks instead of an eagle that soars. Those words are not the truth. They may have come from your dad telling you that you will never amount to anything or that you just don't have what it takes. That you will never be the man your brother is. Or it can be what you say negative to yourself all the time. Whatever those words may be or have been to smother you and lie to you and make you crawl in a hole, it is all a lie. Do not let this destroy or steal your heart the rest of your days.

The LORD is close to the broken hearted and saves those who are crushed in spirit. —Psalm 34:18

He is close to you. Give Him your wounded heart, He will and can stop the bleeding.

YOU ARE CONSIDERED A DANGEROUS AND MAJOR THREAT TO THE KINGDOM OF DARKNESS.

WHAT'S COMING OUT OF YOUR MOUTH

I want to touch on what is proceeding out of your mouth. I don't believe it is talked about enough and I don't believe you may understand where things in your life may be coming from. I trust that once you see this, you will make the changes needed in your own life. Check this out...I gave you the first part of this earlier talking about bullying...but keep reading the rest of this...

> *But the things that proceed out of the mouth come from the heart, and those defile the man. For out of the heart come evil thoughts, murders, adulteries, fornications, thefts, false witness, slanders. These are the things that defile the man...* —Matthew 15:18-20a (NASB)

This Scripture is saying that what comes out of a man's mouth says everything of what is going on in his heart. Get this...a lot of times you can see what a man's heart is by the way he talks. This obviously includes the girls, but I'm just keying in on you gentlemen right now. What is coming out of your mouth to others? Can people count on you to be honest and truthful? Not someone who lies or exaggerates the truth. It also says where evil thoughts and sexual immorality is coming from—the heart. Slandering people, talking down to them is coming from—the heart. Bullying kids is coming from—the heart. Are you a bully? A bully has a heart issue. When you stop to open a door for a woman at the mall, it comes from—the heart. When you tell the truth when you could easily tell a lie instead, it comes from—the heart. When you honor a young lady you are dating when you could take advantage of her, it comes from—the heart.

So you see...the hidden man of the heart is very powerful. Who are you within your heart? You will have your answer when you listen to what is coming out of your mouth and from the actions of your life. As a warrior within, I challenge you to make the changes needed in this area of what is coming out of your mouth.

HIS VOICE

> *"Then you will call upon Me and come and pray to Me, and I will listen to you. You will seek Me and find Me when you search for Me with all your heart. I will be found by you," declares the* LORD... —Jeremiah 29:12-14a (NASB)

As you are going after and growing into a warrior within, you want to be able to know the voice of God and be led by His direction. Jesus often would go to a quiet place and spend time with the Father. That's why He could choose the 12 disciples, turn water into wine, raise Lazarus from the dead, feed 5,000 people and on it goes. All of what Jesus did was from going to God in prayer.

It is imperative that you have a personal relationship with Jesus. That means taking the time to get to know Him. There are a lot of Christian young people who do not have this quiet time and there are a lot of them who do. It takes discipline, time, a place to go, and a heart willing to be obedient to how God will direct your steps. It strengthens your authority in Him so that you can be that leader that many want to stand alongside. It's an exciting way to live as the Lord is very adventurous and will take you to places you never thought in a million years you could ever go...but you need to hear Him.

YOU MUST MAKE YOUR QUIET TIME WITH HIM A PRIORITY.

Maybe this will help you to see the importance of having personal time with the Lord daily. Let me ask you, if you work out with weights to get stronger and build muscle, can you just do that for one or two days, or one or two weeks and get the results you were hoping for? No, that would be foolish to think that. You have to lift different weights daily to get the results you want to build muscle and become stronger. Well, this is the exact same thing. To build spiritual muscle and get stronger, you must take the time daily to spend time with the Lord. When you see strong men of God that you look up to, I guarantee you they are in His Word and praying every day to stay in relationship with the Lord. There is no relationship without communication. That is true within your own life of friends and family. It is the same with the Lord...no relationship without spending time.

There will always be many things competing for your attention in life—family, friends, jobs, school work, social media, entertainment, even youth group. In the midst of all of this, where do you place Jesus? It's possible to lose focus on your relationship with Him. But when you realize He literally is your lifeline – that line of rescue and a place to secure yourself to Him, you will enjoy a relationship like none other.

So how do you do this? Here are a few tools/ways to begin the habit of a personal quiet time. Know that there is no formula to this, but that it is something you can use to draw close to the Lord and find an intimate relationship with the God of the universe. If you miss a day or so, just get back on track again…no worries.

In becoming a warrior within, you must make your quiet time with Him a priority. You will see when you make Him the priority how so many things in your life will come into order. For Jesus promised, *"Seek first the kingdom of God and His righteousness, and all these things will be added to you."* Matthew 6:33 (NASB). So here we go…

WHAT IS NEEDED TO SET UP A PERSONAL QUIET TIME

1. **Pick a set time—and stick to it.** Most people like to do this early in the morning, some like before going to bed. Whichever is your choice…start with 15 minutes. It will challenge you to no longer pick up your phone to look at social media first thing in the morning or right before going to bed. It will be a sacrifice, a discipline, but that's what is needed as a warrior. You will see how quickly that 15 minutes will become half an hour or longer as you start drawing close to the Lord.

2. **Have a specific place—and stick to it.** Find a place that is comfortable for you to set yourself apart unto God for this time. Do not use your bed…you will find yourself quickly falling asleep. Get out of bed—go to another room in the house; sit on the floor in your room; find a place that is quiet. You will need to turn off your phone, as that is the #1 distraction for everyone. You can also use your notebook to write down anything that comes up in your mind that you need to do that day or the next day. In writing it down you will no longer be thinking about it during your prayer time. Get to that specific place daily—you have an appointment with God.

3. **Have a Bible and a notebook.** I highly suggest you go old school and have a Bible with you. Not using an electronic Bible so you are not distracted to look at your phone, computer, Ipad, etc. Have a

notebook with you so when something you read pops out to you, you can write it out and begin to ask the Lord what it means. This is a sure way you will begin to hear His voice—through His Word.

4. **Use ACTS – Adoration, Confession, Thanksgiving, Supplication.** Once you are in that quiet place, you can use these four ways to pray, talk to, and communicate with the Lord.

> **Adoration – This is praise and worship.** Begin by praising the Lord and worshipping Him for Who He is. This is by far the greatest weapon in your arsenal. Satan hates when you praise God. He hates that you acknowledge Jesus as Lord. Satan was the music director in heaven, he understands worship, he wants praised, he hates that your allegiance is to the Most High God. In knowing that, praise the Lord even louder! Something like: "God, You are all knowing, you are faithful, your wisdom is sure, you are without measure, you are the beginning and end of all things, you are majestic and holy, you do not lie, all you promised you will do, you can be trusted, I am grateful for you are merciful, actively compassionate in my life. You are gracious and enjoy giving great gifts to your kids. You see how you can go on and on. Thank Him. Praise Him. Worship Him. Speak all of this out loud. And sing!! Find great worship music to sing along with or make up your own tune…but sing. That will cause every enemy of your soul to flee, bringing the peace and comfort of God Most High.

> **Confession – daily.** This is simply confessing to the Lord things you may have said, done, a bad habit, anything you sense in your heart that you need to confess before the Lord. Own this. Take responsibility for that which is trying to keep you from Him. He is not mad at you. He loves you. He already knows. Just go to Him, confess it, ask the Lord to forgive you, receive His forgiveness and move on in prayer. "*…as far as the east is from the west, so far has He removed our transgressions from us*" (Psalm 103:12). What a promise…believe Him.

> **Thanksgiving.** No bigger tool than thanksgiving. When you have a grateful heart, no matter what is going on in your life,

you will receive great peace from His heart to yours. When you can say, "I trust you and I thank you for showing me a way through this", you put the responsibility on the Lord to see you through that situation good or bad. This certainly can be hard to do at times, but a thankful heart releases the burden of a heavy heart. Here is where you can pray for friends, family, your future bride, situations at school. Thank Him for His blessings, for showing you ways to pray, praying for the needs of others. *"Give thanks with a grateful heart."*

Supplications – your personal requests to the Lord. After you have worshipped the Lord, confessed your sins, and given thanks, now you can ask on behalf of yourself and others. This obviously is where you ask the Lord for your needs, heart's desires, mercy, healing of a wounded heart. Whatever you are going through, tell Him. He hears you. Be honest. This is where you will grow so much when you are honest in talking to Him and He in return will make your relationship with Him very real. *"Ask and it will be given to you; seek and you will find; knock and the door will be opened to you."* This is the heart of God...He wants to give you good gifts that will bless you and bring you great joy. Ask Him. No matter what, He loves you anyway. It is His good pleasure to bless you! Ask...

The voice of God can be found. It is like all relationships; you need to spend time. You just need to sit quiet long enough to hear what the spirit of the Lord is saying to just you. He is personal. He knows you far more than you know yourself. The only thing that truly blesses Him is a relationship with you. Think about that – God, the Savior of the World, the Holy Spirit wants a close, intimate relationship with you. Your name is known in heaven: *"I have redeemed you; I have summoned you by name; you are mine"* (Isaiah 43:1b).

YOUR NAME IS KNOWN IN HEAVEN

HIS WARRIOR/HIS LEADER

When I was a child, I spoke as a child, I thought like a child, I reasoned like a child. When I became a man, I put aside childish things.
—1 Corinthians 13:11 (NASB)

As I have been saying this entire book, you have been called and challenged to be a warrior for your generation. With that call is a huge responsibility as a man of integrity, character, and strength. In the Scripture above, you are challenged to put away childish things and step out into the adventure ahead of being the man God has always called you to be.

In this segment, and because this book is on standing strong in a reckless world, I want to take two men from the Bible who were strong men of God. Who were called to their destiny at a young age. Who were chosen to be leaders and warriors of their time. Two different guys had the same familiar circumstances in leadership and with women, but their choices were completely different. I write these because I want you to see the choice for sexual pleasure is as ancient as the bible days. Which makes the Bible quite relevant. These two characters, Joseph and Samson, were real people, living in real times, paving a way with stories for us to glean from.

In looking at these two men, you will see what it takes to be a leader. The sacrifice it takes. The obedience that is necessary. And how one saw many years of victory in his journey, and the other died young because of his lack of integrity and character. I think you will see how similar they are and then see how polar opposites they are.

So buckle up—and get a hold of these examples of these men and make your choice of what kind of man you want to be...in the area of sexual integrity.

JOSEPH

Genesis 37:5-36; 39: 1-18; 40-46 – I am going to paraphrase this story, you can read it later on your own.

Joseph grew up the favored son of his father Jacob. He had two dreams as a young man that he would rule over his family. When he told his brothers and parents these dreams, his brothers became angry and jealous of him. Jacob, his father, also rebuked his dreams but Jacob also "pondered it all in his mind."

Because of their hate and jealousy for their younger brother, Joseph's brothers sold him as a slave to a caravan heading to Egypt. They stripped him of his coat of many colors that his dad gave him, killed a goat and dipped his coat in goat's blood and told their father that Joseph was killed by a ferocious animal. Think about that for a second, they watched their father grieve over the death of his son, but that son was alive and well. (That's a whole other story—at another time.) But think about the hateful heart of those brothers to do something like that to their dad.

Joseph was taken to Egypt as a slave and brought into the house of Potiphar, an Egyptian officer of Pharaoh. Joseph was very successful in Potiphar's home as a servant and has much, much favor with God. Because of Joseph's character and strength of leadership and the hand of the Lord on his life, Potiphar trusted him and made him his personal servant; later he made Joseph the overseer over his house and all that he owned. Obviously, Potiphar really trusted Joseph with everything in his home and was not concerned about anything. The Bible tells us that Joseph was handsome in form and appearance. Obviously it means he was not only handsome, he was built pretty strong as well. As the girls would say, "he was hot."

Now here is the part of this story of Joseph's choice that I want you to see—Genesis 39:7 states that Potiphar's wife looked with desire at Joseph, and she said, "Lie with me." No different then when a girl is luring you.

Joseph refused and said to his master's wife that his master had trusted him with everything in his house. That Potiphar had made no one greater in the house than Joseph. That Potiphar had withheld nothing from him except her, because she was his wife. And the best line Joseph gave, "How then could I do this great evil and sin against God?"

There is his "5-second decision." There is his sexual integrity/character. There is the warrior within.

It goes on to say that she asked him to lie with her "day after day." She is coming onto him every single day trying to break him down to sleep with her…day after day. The temptation was every day. Think about that… every single day. Certainly he thought about it. Certainly he desired it.

Certainly he knew that no one would know. But, (when you see the word but, pay attention with what comes next), Joseph had made up in his mind and heart that he was not going to sin against his boss but more than that against God.

It says that "on one particular day," Potiphar's wife waited until there were no men in the house and grabbed him by his garment and said, "Lie with me!" (There is an exclamation point in a few Bible versions I am using, so that says to me she was insistent). When she grabbed him by his garment, "he left his garment in her hand and fled, and went outside." This is self-control and self-denial under great, great temptation.

As the story goes, Potiphar's wife screamed and said that Joseph tried to rape her and her proof was Joseph's garment in her hand. When Potiphar found out, he became angry and threw him in jail. Joseph was in prison for many years. To make this long and amazing story short, the Lord found favor with Joseph again, and he served as second in command to Pharoah. He married and had two sons. Because of his character, leadership and integrity, Joseph saved Israel from a terrible famine and was reconciled to his family. The dream he had as a kid came to pass beyond his wildest dreams.

YOU CAN'T PUT A PRICE TAG ON
OBEDIENCE AND HONOR.

So learn and take note of this story. Joseph was a man of valor, honor, trust, sexual integrity and great character. That did not stop him from being tempted beyond what most men are. Actually he paid a price for something he never did. Way above what I am sure he ever thought would happen to him. But what it did do is show us that his heart, leadership and integrity made this wise young man into an example for you to learn from. To deny his own pleasure for the sake of honoring God is a cut above the rest. It is a challenge that is set before you. I am most assured that it was not easy for him to do. It won't be easy for you to do either. *But you can't put a price tag on obedience and honor.* It's who you become as you serve the Lord and become His warrior. He will see to it that you are blessed in return.

Draw from this story. There is so much more here to learn from. Read it on your own. Now let's look at Samson.

SAMSON

Judges 13-16 – I am going to paraphrase this story as well, you can read it on your own.

Samson was born after an angel of the Lord appeared to his mom and told her that she would have a son. That this boy was going to be a Nazarite, set apart to God from birth, and he would deliver Israel from the Philistines. So, before he was even born, Samson's destiny was set for him. He was chosen by God to defeat the Philistines. As a Nazarite, he was not allowed to drink wine or any alcoholic drink; could not eat anything unclean; and no razor could be used on his head. (No haircuts!)

In reading this entire story, it is obvious from the beginning that Samson was defiant and disobedient even though the Spirit of the Lord was on him. Read on.

When Samson was a young man, he saw a young Philistine girl. He told his parents, "now get her for me as my wife." His parents tried to convince him not to marry a girl from their enemy, the Philistines, but he insisted and demanded, "get her for me." Whenever you insist on having your own way, wanting what you want, when you want it, no matter what advice you get from others, you are in trouble. You will see a pattern here with Samson and the way he deals with his life.

When Samson and his parents were traveling to the town where this girl was, a lion came roaring toward him. The Spirit of the Lord came on him in power, and he tore the lion apart. Think about that! Do you realize the power behind a roaring lion coming at you? Here Samson was tearing it apart with his bare hands. Crazy strength...crazy power! The Lord had given him such strength.

But watch this...after a while Samson saw the carcass of the lion. In it was a swarm of bees and some honey, which he scooped out with his hand and ate as he was walking. Then, when he rejoined his parents, he gave them some. But he did not tell them he had taken the honey from the lion's carcass. As a Nazarite, Samson was not supposed to eat something unclean that had touched a dead animal. But Samson didn't care. Here he was, again, doing what he wanted, when he wanted. But now he had involved other people. You will never be reckless alone. Once you start on this path of dishonor and disrespect for those around you, you will start dragging others through the mud with you.

Samson had no respect for his Nazarite vow. He had no respect for the power of God in his life or he wouldn't have defiled it. Do you see the opposites in Samson and Joseph? Joseph was being led by the Lord, but he did it with integrity and character. Samson was being led by the Lord, but he was reckless, prideful, and couldn't care less about his character before God.

Samson had a sensual lust that controlled him his whole life.

The rest of this story is too long for details, but Samson was no longer married to the first girl. One day, Samson went to Gaza where he saw a prostitute. He spent the night with her. Again, doing what he wanted, when he wanted, with whomever he wanted. His lust controlled him. After being with this prostitute, he met Delilah. The Bible says that he fell in love with her. I don't believe Samson knew what love was. He was so reckless with every part of his life that it seemed that when he tired of someone or something, he moved on.

There was no integrity, no character. Samson used his strength as a sport rather than taking it seriously as a gift the Lord had given him to fulfill his destiny. Because he wouldn't control his lust for women, he finally met his fate with Delilah.

When the rulers of the Philistines realized that Samson was at Delilah's house, they asked her to lure him into telling her where his strength came from. They would pay her silver for the information. She didn't hesitate… she was willing to do whatever they wanted. He may have been in love with her, but she was obviously not feeling the same way. And because he was so used to having what he wanted with whomever he wanted, he didn't recognize she was willing to throw him to the lions so to speak.

Delilah continued asking Samson where his strength came from. He gave her many answers, but he was not telling her the truth. He lied to her over and over. He was playing around with the gift God had given him. And every time she did what he said to reveal his strength, she cried, "Samson, the Philistines are upon you." Each time he broke loose. Do you see his arrogance? His pride? He was making a joke and a mockery of the Lord's gift and calling. You know that Scripture, "pride comes before a fall?" Watch this...

With much nagging, she prodded him day after day after day until he was tired to death according to Judges 16:16. Look at this! Samson was nagged day after day after day, and he was so tired of it he decided to tell her the truth. It was his uncut hair that gave him is strength. Joseph was also nagged day after day after day...but instead of giving in he ran away. There is a huge difference between these men in integrity, character, and honoring God.

After Samson fell asleep, Delilah called a man to shave off the seven braids of his hair, and his strength left him. She called out to him again to tell him the Philistines were upon him. Here is the saddest Scripture in the Bible..."He woke from his sleep and thought, 'I'll go out as before and shake myself free.' But, *"he did not know the LORD had left him."*

OUR CULTURE IS ALSO LURING SO MANY
CHRISTIAN YOUNG MEN TO SLEEP

Here was a man full of all the promises of God, called by God from a young age, gifted by God at a young age. But because he could never, or chose never, to control the lust of his heart, the lust of his eyes, he had fallen so far from becoming the man he was called to be that he no longer recognized that the Lord had left him.

Today, our culture is also luring so many Christian young men to sleep, to follow after the lust of their eyes and the lust of their flesh. It is causing them to lose sight of the warrior that desperately wants to be released.

Back to Samson… After they cut his hair, they gouged out his eyes, bound him with shackles and led him to prison. But the hair on his head began to grow back again, and his strength secretly returned. When the Philistines brought him out to their arena to make "sport of him," he asked the servant there to put him between the two pillars that supported the Philistine temple. Then Samson cried out to God to remember him and give him his strength just once more. He put his hands on the two pillars, pushed on them and the entire place fell down killing more Philistines when Samson died than when he lived.

There is much to say about living a life on your terms instead of on God's terms. I challenge you that it may seem fun to do whatever you want, whenever you want, but there is a price to pay in living that way. Take note also, Samson did ask for forgiveness and God did forgive him and allow him to finish his task in defeating the Philistines just as God had ordained him to do.

I love these stories because these men were strong leaders, courageous, and called by God. But they both had a choice on how they were going to lead others and be obedient to the call on their lives. This is no different than the call of God on your life. Glean from these stories. They were written just for you.

After reading about these two men, who would you follow? Be honest. Which one would you want your life to follow? And once you choose your answer, would you be the kind of leader and warrior that you would want to follow? Great question. (You can answer these at the end of this chapter in the Take Action section.)

LOOK ONE MORE TIME

I didn't want to leave this most important tool in your life out of this book. This is something that is your lifeline. You are as close to Him as you want to be. It is up to you whether you hold a hand up to reject Him, or you draw near to Him and let Him draw near to you. He wants to be very close to you. He has said that to mankind all through the Scriptures. Prayer is very important in your walk with the Lord. Prayer is simply talking to God. It is open communication, a give and take conversation, between you and the Lord. I believe, because I know it works, if you take the time to do this in your life, on a daily basis, you will find so many answers to questions and the Lord will lead you to His purposes not your purposes for your life. You will watch how He will direct your path. You will experience the peace that will set in your heart. You will come to know with your heart, not just with your head, that you have a friend in Jesus. And that He sticks closer than a brother.

I am telling you this as a sister in the Lord, you will grow leaps and bounds in your walk with Him if you will take the time to meet with him every morning. Let's do this hypothetical question…if you knew that Selena Gomez was going to call you every morning at 6:00 a.m., would you get up to answer the phone and talk to her?) (Or you can put whatever famous person you would really like to talk to that you may never get the chance to do so in there)…but get the point? If you would wake up for Selena or a famous person, then why would you not wake up for the Savior of the entire Universe, who is the only One who knows you fully and who has your purpose all laid out, who looks forward to being with you and who is waiting on you every morning?!! Think about that! You have an appointment with God every morning. Will you keep that appointment?!

The effectual prayer of a righteous man can accomplish much.
—James 5:16

IT'S YOUR TURN

Take the time to think about these questions from Chapter Five. Your answers will help you in making clear and wise decisions for yourself. Don't skip this. This is your life. Take the time to make the changes in this area of sexual integrity.

JOURNAL: CHAPTER FIVE

How can you begin to be a voice of authority, reason and truth for your generation? The voice speaking life through strength of the truth?

_____

_____

_____

_____

_____

_____

_____

Who are you as a hidden man of the heart?

_____

_____

_____

_____

_____

_____

_____

After knowing the downfall of so many things in King David's life that the Lord knew he was going to do, what made the Lord still call him "a man after His heart"? Do you see the Lord saying that to you?

Have you ever heard the Lord speak to your heart? Do you believe God wants to have that kind of relationship with you?

You know that there is no formula to have a personal quiet time with the Lord. But it's important to pray and meet with him daily. Did the information given on how to have this personal time helpful for you to get started? How?

_____

_____

_____

_____

_____

_____

TAKE ACTION:

If you find it hard to sit quietly before the Lord for at least 15 minutes a day at the start, what is distracting you? How would you fix it so that you can take that time?

_____

_____

_____

_____

_____

_____

What was the biggest difference between Joseph and Samson that you saw? And if their stories resonated with you, how?

Right now in your life, are you the kind of leader and warrior that you would want to follow? What is the first thing that you need to change?

NOT UP FOR DEBATE

Flee sexual immorality. All other sins a man commits are outside his body, but he who sins sexually sins against his own body.
—1 Corinthians 6:18

I don't know how often you have been told about Sexually Transmitted Diseases, but I want, once again, to give you an understanding of why you don't want to take this lightly. Now that we've reached this segment, I pray that you are convinced that God intended sexual pleasure to be solely for marriage. When God created man and woman, it was never His intention that they would share their bodies with so many other people. That is why there is disease related to sexual promiscuity. Our bodies were never meant to be shared with one person after another.

There is such an epidemic in our culture of STDs all because society insists on doing what is right in their own eyes.

This chapter is a little heavy. It is always difficult to expose things that cause heartache and pain. But I don't want to shy away from truth.

OUR BODIES WERE NEVER MEANT TO BE SHARED
WITH ONE PERSON AFTER ANOTHER.

SAFE SEX?

If you listen to the media and many people in the educational system, they would have you believe that if you just use a condom, everything will be ok. Why is it that when someone gives you that kind of advice, it is never 100% full proof?

Yes, condoms are marketed as a form of birth control. They are marketed to protect from STDs, **but** none of that protection is certain. The question becomes, why would anyone choose something that is not 100% sure and call it safe or responsible?

The answer is that adult "experts" are so convinced that you couldn't possibly control yourself and choose God's way (it's too old-fashioned and unheard of in this century) that they use safe sex through condoms as a band-aid on this subject. If this is the answer, then why do the statistics show that 1 in 4 teenagers gets an STD a year? (Center for Disease Control and Prevention) It is a battle that teens are losing.

I have another question for the "experts": "who has the condom for teenagers' hearts and their emotions"? (We'll get to that in a minute)

I did much of my research through the Center for Disease Control (CDC). The CDC recommends using a condom while engaging in sex outside of marriage. **However,** (pay attention) in _every_ case when describing each STD, they have determined that the greatest protection against any sexual disease is abstinence, or having only one partner. Again it is such a lie to tell you to use a condom and you are protected all the time. That is not true. And having multiple partners will expose you to more than double the risk of an STD.

Now, if they, as a national health program, know what will keep you the safest, why isn't that message heard loud and clear everywhere else? Abstinence is not a safe sex _option_. It's the safe sex _answer_.

Think of it this way, would you let your best friend who was drunk get behind the wheel of their car and say to them, "just put on your seatbelt, you'll be safe enough?" What is safe enough? The hope is that you won't be in an accident and kill yourself or others? You know you would never do that. I'm sure you've heard the slogan that says, "friends don't let friends drive drunk." Then why the double standard regarding sex and condoms? Think about it.

There were a group of doctors at a convention talking about STDs and the HIV virus. As the experts, they were recommending getting the condom message out especially to teens to prevent disease among this generation. When asked which doctor would use a condom if their partner had HIV, not one of them raised their hand to say they would! So, they won't do what they are telling you to do. So you see, man is trying to keep these diseases from getting so out of control that they are telling you to use a condom. It's like playing Russia roulette—you have no idea when that bullet will be in the chamber. Same with the safe sex message, you never know when it will work and when it won't.

You are going to be married one day. Do you honestly want to pass this part of you to her? You must think about all of this and stop living like you don't have a future in front of you.

WATCH OVER YOUR HEART

Emotional scars from sexual activity outside the marriage bed are very rarely spoken of, yet it is the reason so many girls and guys are depressed and overwhelmed within. How can we ignore that place in each of your hearts, acting like it's no big deal, and "I can handle this?" As much as everyone wants you to indulge in sexual activity whenever you want and with whomever you want, no one has the cure for the broken heart.

Emotional scars and pain can last a long time. It is naïve to think otherwise. I have spoken to hundreds and hundreds of teenagers who were emotionally scarred because of the heartache they felt from sexual promiscuity. You give a piece of yourself to someone, and then you walk away from it. That can't keep going on without causing great havoc within your heart.

Watch over [guard] your heart with all diligence, for from it flows the spring of life.   —Proverbs 4:23

Life comes from the heart. Your heart is being affected. When a teenage girl or guy engages in sexual promiscuity and continues to do whatever they want and feel no remorse, it is a great indication their heart has become callous and hard and no longer senses the warning in their conscience and spirit that they are on a downward spiral. If this is you or someone you know, talk to a youth pastor or pastor. You don't want this kind of heart… it will steal every good thing away from you.

It is not a joke when guys brag about how many girls they have had and that they couldn't care less. It can no longer be denied or hidden that the emotional aspect of sexual sin is being left out. I challenge each of you to come to the table and find your greatest hope of freedom for your heart when you allow the Lord to come into those places and touch you with His strength, power, grace and love.

TEEN PREGNANCY - A HEARTBEAT AWAY

Teen pregnancy and abortion, a topic that never involves the guys input or his feelings. You never hear about what the boy wants in this situation. We always just hear that it is all about the girls, their feelings and what they want to do with this very difficult situation because it's her body. I do not agree with that. You have a responsibility in this as well. Understand, both of these situations will change your life forever. I am sure many of you may know someone your age who has had a child out of wedlock or an abortion, and you have watched them struggle through both of those situations. I have sat, listened to, cried with and counseled many teenage girls and a few boys through both. The heartache and tears were always overwhelming as they were dealing with the emotional exhaustion that someone their age never should have been in a position to deal with.

Realize that the only reason your generation is in these situations is because the real choice started when teens decided to sleep with their boyfriends/girlfriends. That was the first choice, the "5-second decision"…and then the choices kept mounting once a pregnancy was involved. It is not an easy road if you are involved in a teen pregnancy. It not only involves you, your girlfriend and the baby, but both families. God's grace, love, forgiveness and mercy has helped many through these overwhelming situations.

If you know of someone who is in this circumstance, please encourage them to seek help through the Crisis Pregnancy Center near them. They will give support, encouragement, resources and great godly counseling. They will help families make wise choices of saving a beating heart. The gift of life hangs in the balance with these situations of teen pregnancy and abortion.

IT IS NOT AN EASY ROAD IF YOU ARE INVOLVED IN A TEEN PREGNANCY.

AN UNDENIABLY INTIMATE SEXUAL ACT

I must also address the subject of oral sex. Somehow, in some way, someone has convinced your entire generation that oral sex isn't sex. That it's ok because you are still a virgin.

Let me reassure you that *oral sex is an undeniably intimate sexual act*. It is every bit as sexually intimate as intercourse. And a virgin, as Webster's Dictionary states, is a man or woman who hasn't had sexual intercourse, **and also**, one who is free of impurity or stain. So yes, technically you are holding onto your virginity, **but** you are also sexually active and therefore sexually impure.

You cannot be confused with this. As I said in Chapter 2 with friends with benefits, it is a sexual act used by most boys for self-gratification from a girl whether they know them or not. A way to have broken pieces of your heart everywhere. *"....Or do you not know that your body is a temple of the Holy Spirit who is in you, whom you have from God, and that you are not your own? For you have been bought with a price; therefore glorify God in your body"* (1 Corinthians 6:19-20).

Sexual purity is about the whole person. It's about being pure in spirit, soul, and body; along with the physical and spiritual. It's a cop-out, a way of getting around the idea of sexual integrity, by saying "Oh, this doesn't really matter, it's not really sex, or at least it's not intercourse."

SEXUAL INTEGRITY IS ALL OF YOU, NOT JUST PIECES OF YOU.

Oral sex through friends with benefits is a twisted lie, one that can cause the same damage as intercourse in your emotions, spirit, and physical body. Yes, you most certainly can get an STD being involved in oral sex, especially when many partners are involved. They are finding more STDs in the mouths of guys and girls because of this. Trying to justify it as being ok is a false argument before God. He can't condone that; God is not buying into the cheap lie that has caused so many of His sons to use His daughters, in depraving their heart, mind, and spirit. Sexual integrity is all of you, not just pieces of you.

So I tell you this, and insist on it in the Lord, that you must no longer live as the Gentiles do, in the futility of their thinking...Having lost all sensitivity, they have given themselves over to sensuality so as to indulge in every kind of impurity, with a continual lust for more....But among you there must not be even a hint of sexual immorality, or of any kind of impurity, or of greed, because these are improper for God's holy people....For you were once darkness, but now you are light in the Lord. Live as children of light.... —Ephesians 4:17, 19, 5:3, 8

So please understand that oral sex is sex and even though the world is screaming at your generation that it is no big deal because it's not really sex, it continues to be the lie keeping young people in darkness and their hearts far away from sexual integrity.

A SILENT EPIDEMIC

Sexually Transmitted Diseases can be a silent epidemic. A guy or a girl may never know they have an STD which in the long run can cause a lot of physical problems for them down the road. That's what makes STDs so dangerous. I chose to take the following material directly from the Center of Disease Control Fact Sheets. This information is given to you to give clear understanding of what is going on with your body when disease has taken over.

All of the information from the Center of Disease Control is below. Please read all of the facts that you need to adhere to. I also am giving you how it effects girls too. That way you understand this is hurting both of you. And can have lasting consequences for you. There is a lot to read here, but don't skip this...educate yourself on this matter!

CENTER FOR DISEASE CONTROL FACT SHEET
DON'T SKIP READING ANY OF THIS!

While updating the information for this book, I found the most recent statistics that I am putting in here first.

From the Center for Disease Control so far in 2018, nearly 2.3 million US cases of syphilis, gonorrhea and chlamydia were diagnosed. That's the highest number ever reported nationwide, breaking the record set in 2016 by more than 200,000 cases, according to the CDC. We are talking about millions of infections with just these three diseases.

Why is this getting so bad? Because there are too many people sharing their bodies sexually with so many partners, causing disease to infect millions of people. There are between 27-30 diseases that they know of. I am giving you the most common.

If no one else is sounding this alarm to you, then I will. The cultural fight in this battle is sliding backwards. In trying to stop this pace of disease, you have been told to use a condom and then just do what you want. Obviously, it's not working.

I pray that when you read all that these diseases entail, it will confirm your decision to wait until marriage. You want and need to be informed of what these diseases do to both girls and guys. This is the truth about what happens when people do what is right in their own eyes.

Isn't it amazing, the very thing that God freely created for our pleasure has come with a very costly price outside of His plan.

THE CULTURAL FIGHT IN THIS BATTLE
IS SLIDING BACKWARDS.

CHLAMYDIA

What is Chlamydia?

Chlamydia, which remains the most common STD reported to the CDC, is easily transmitted during any form of sexual activity. If not treated, chlaymdia can lead to pelvic inflammatory disease in women, which can cause permanent damage to the reproductive system. In men, the infection can spread to the tube that carries sperm from the testicles, causing pain and fever. Chlamydia is the most frequently reported bacterial sexually transmitted disease in the United States. In 2006, 1,030,911 chlamydia infections were reported to the CDC from 50 states. An estimated 2,291,000 U.S. civilians ages 14-39 are infected with chlamydia today based on the U.S. National Health and Nutrition Examination Survey.

Chlamydia can be transmitted during vaginal, anal, or oral sex. Chlamydia can also be passed from an infected mother to her baby during vaginal childbirth. Any sexually active person can be infected with chlamydia. The greater the number of sex partners, the greater the risk of infection.

Chlamydia is known as a "silent" disease because about three quarters of infected women and about half of infected men have no symptoms. If untreated, chlamydia infections can progress to serious reproductive and other health problems with both short-term and long-term consequences. Like the disease itself, the damage that chlamydia causes is often "silent." In women, untreated infection can spread into the uterus or fallopian tubes and cause pelvic inflammatory disease (PID). This happens in up to 40 percent of women with untreated chlamydia. PID can cause permanent damage to the fallopian tubes, uterus, and surrounding tissues.

Babies who are born to infected mothers can get chlamydial infections in their eyes and respiratory tracts. Chlamydia is a leading cause of early infant pneumonia and pink eye in newborns.

Chlamydia can be easily treated and cured with antibiotics. However, persons with chlamydia should abstain from sexual intercourse until they and their sex partners have completed treatment, otherwise re-infection is possible. Having multiple infections increases a woman's risk of serious reproductive health complications, including infertility.

The surest way to avoid transmission of STDs is to abstain from sexual contact, or to be in a long-term mutually monogamous relationship. In other words, abstain till marriage.

HPV

What is HPV?

Genital human papillomavirus (HPV) is one of the most common sexually transmitted infections. There are more than 40 HPV types that can infect the genital area of men and women. You cannot see HPV. Most people who become infected with HPV do not even know they have it.

Most people with HPV do not develop symptoms or health problems. But sometimes, certain types of HPV can cause genital warts in men and women. Other HPV types can cause cervical cancer and other less common cancers, such as cancers of the vulva, vagina, anus, throat and penis. The types of HPV that can cause genital warts are not the same as the types that can cause cancer.

Genital warts usually appear as small bumps or groups of bumps, usually in the genital area. Warts may appear within weeks or months after sexual contact with an infected person. Medical treatment is required to remove them (it often takes multiple visits).

For those who choose to be sexually active, condoms may lower the risk of HPV, if used all the time and in the right way. Condoms may also lower the risk of developing HPV related diseases, such as genital warts and cervical cancer. But HPV can infect areas that are not covered by a condom – so condoms may not fully protect against HPV. So the only sure way to prevent HPV is to avoid sexual activity before marriage.

There is no treatment for the virus itself...visible genital warts can be removed by patient-applied medications, or treated by a health care provider. Some individuals choose to forego treatment to see if the warts will disappear on their own. No one treatment is better than another. Cervical cancer is most easily treatable when it is diagnosed and treated early. But women who get routine Pap testing and follow up as needed can identify problems before cancer develops. Prevention is always better than treatment.

The surest way to avoid transmission of STDs is to abstain from sexual contact, or to be in a long-term mutually monogamous relationship with a partner who has been tested and is known to be uninfected.

GONORRHEA

What is Gonorrhea?

Gonorrhea is a sexually transmitted disease (STD). Gonorrhea is caused by Neisseria gonorrhoeae, a bacterium that can grow and multiply easily in the warm, moist areas of the reproductive tract, including the cervix (opening to the womb), uterus (womb), and fallopian tubes (egg canals) in women, and in the urethra (urine canal) in women and men. The bacterium can also grow in the mouth, throat, eyes, and anus.

Gonorrhea is a very common sexually infectious disease. CDC estimates that more than 700,000 persons in the U.S. get new gonorrheal infections each year. Only about half of these infections are reported to CDC.

Gonorrhea is spread through contact with the penis, vagina, mouth or anus. Gonorrhea can also be spread from mother to baby during delivery.

People who have had gonorrhea and received treatment may get infected again if they have sexual contact with a person infected with gonorrhea.

Gonorrhea is also known as a "silent" disease because any sexually active person can be infected with gonorrhea. In the United States, the highest reported rates of infection are among sexually active teenagers and young adults.

The initial symptoms and signs in women include a painful or burning sensation when urinating, increased vaginal discharge, or vaginal bleeding between periods. Women with gonorrhea are at risk of developing serious complications from the infection, regardless of the presence or severity of symptoms.

The symptoms in men, if not treated, can cause severe and permanent health issues, including problems with the prostate and testicles.

Several antibiotics can successfully cure gonorrhea in adolescents and adults. However, drug-resistant strains of gonorrhea are increasing in many parts of the world including the United States, and successful treatment of gonorrhea is becoming more difficult. Because many people with gonorrhea also have chlamydia, antibiotics for both infections are usually given together.

The surest way to avoid transmission of STDs is to abstain from sexual intercourse, or to be in a long-term mutually monogamous relationship with a partner who has been tested and is known to be uninfected.

GENITAL HERPES

What is Genital Herpes?

Genital herpes is a sexually transmitted disease (STD) caused by the herpes simplex viruses type 1 (HSV-1) or type 2 (HSV-2). Most genital herpes are caused by HSV-2. Most individuals have no or only minimal signs or symptoms from HSV-1 or HSV-2 infection. When signs do occur, they typically appear as one or more blisters on or around the genitals or rectum. The blisters break, leaving tender ulcers (sores) that may take two to four weeks to heal the first time they occur. Typically, another outbreak can appear weeks or months after the first, but it almost always is less severe and shorter than the first outbreak. Although the infection can stay in the body indefinitely, the number of outbreaks may decrease over a period of years.

Nationwide, at least 45 million people ages 12 and older, or one out of five adolescents and adults, have had genital HSV infection. Over the past decade, the percent of Americans with genital herpes infection in the U.S. has decreased.

Generally, a person can get HSV-2 infection during sexual contact with someone who has genital HSVC-2 infection. Transmission can occur from an infected partner who does not have a visible sore and may not know that he or she is infected.

HSV-1 can cause genital herpes, but it more commonly causes infections of the mouth and lips, so called "fever blisters." HSV-1 infection of the genitals can be caused by oral-genital or genital-genital contact with a person who has HSV-1 infection. Genital HSV-1 outbreaks recur less regularly than genital HSV-2 outbreaks.

Regardless of the severity of the symptoms, genital herpes frequently causes psychological distress in people who know they are infected.

If a woman has active genital herpes at delivery, a cesarean delivery is usually performed. Fortunately, infection of a baby from a woman with herpes infection is rare.

There is no treatment that can cure this herpes virus...but antiviral medications can shorten and prevent outbreaks during the period of time the person takes the medication.

The surest way to avoid transmission of STDs is to abstain from sexual intercourse, or to be in a long-term mutually monogamous relationship with a partner who has been tested and is known to be uninfected.

HIV/AIDS

What is HIV?

HIV stands for human immunodeficiency virus. This is the virus that causes AIDS. HIV is different from most other viruses because it attacks the immune system. The immune system gives our bodies the ability to fight infections. HIV finds and destroys a type of white blood cell (T cells or CD4 cells) that the immune system must have to fight disease.

AIDS stands for acquired immunodeficiency syndrome. AIDS is the final stage of HIV infection. It can take years for a person infected with HIV, even without treatment, to reach this stage. Having AIDS means that the virus has weakened the immune system to the point at which the body has a difficult time fighting infection. When someone has one or more specific infections, certain cancers, or a very low number of T cells, he/she is considered to have AIDS.

HIV is primarily found in the blood, semen, or vaginal fluid of an infected person. HIV is transmitted in 3 main ways...

+ Having sex (anal, vaginal, or oral) with someone infected with HIV

+ Sharing needles and syringes with someone infected with HIV

+ Being exposed (fetus or infant) to HIV before or during birth or through breast feeding.

The only way to know whether you are infected is to be tested for HIV. You cannot rely on symptoms alone because many people who are infected with HIV do not have symptoms for many years. Someone can look and feel healthy but can still be infected. In fact, one quarter of the HIV-infected persons in the U.S. do not know that they are infected.

Once HIV enters the body, the body starts to produce antibodies— substances the immune system creates after infection. Most HIV tests look for these antibodies rather than the virus itself. There are many different kinds of HIV tests, including rapid tests and home test kits. All HIV tests approved by the U.S. government are very good at diagnosing HIV.

The surest way to avoid transmission of STDs is to abstain from sexual intercourse, or to be in a long-term mutually monogamous relationship with a partner who has been tested and is known to be uninfected.

LOOK ONE MORE TIME!

After you have read all of the information from the Center of Disease Control, look at how many millions of people suffer with a sexually transmitted disease. I trust that you don't want to be included in this statistic. Therefore, you are in a perfect position to make wise and healthy choices for yourself **now** that will positively affect you, your future wife and children later on in life.

You have a marvelous future ahead of you. You are not just living for the now. There is much living to do—and much to enjoy in the relationship that God has ordained for you in the future. But between now and then, you still have a choice to make regarding your relationships. You can choose to do it God's way, or you can choose to do it the world's way. Please note that what God has given so freely, within the boundaries He thought were best, has been warped by a society that wants what it wants, whenever it wants it—but no one wants to pay the price for it! You will always be challenged with living a sexually pure, holy lifestyle, whether married or single. And it all comes down to the issues of the heart. Be diligent to protect and guard your heart.

As water reflects a face, so a man's heart reflects the man.

—Proverbs 27:19

YOU ARE NOT JUST LIVING FOR THE NOW.

IT'S YOUR TURN

Take the time to think about these questions from Chapter Six. Your answers will help you in making clear and wise decisions for yourself. Don't skip this. This is your life. Take the time to make the changes in this area of sexual integrity.

JOURNAL: CHAPTER SIX

What does it mean by the Scripture at the opening of this chapter when it says, *"….he who sins sexually sins against his own body"*? Does that help you to see what the effects of sexual sin can do?

_____

_____

_____

_____

_____

_____

Do you believe that if you just use a condom everything will be ok…no pregnancy, no disease? If so, what facts can you stand on?

_____

_____

_____

_____

_____

_____

_____

If you don't believe that a condom protects you, can you explain in your own words from what you learned in this chapter why and how you can explain it to others?

One more question about safe sex...would you give your best friend who happened to get very drunk at a party, the keys to his car and tell him to drive home but be safe? Why? Why not? Explain. What does that have to do with using a condom?

Really want you to think about this....As much as everyone wants you to indulge in sexual activity, who then has a cure for the broken heart? And how does sexual activity outside of marriage honor God?

TAKE ACTION:

I am not going to ask you a few questions about oral sex. I want, though, to ask you to read the section again under "An Undeniably Intimate Sexual Act," and write out three things you never knew about this sexual act and what you can do to pursue sexual integrity.

You are going to marry one day. Do you honestly want to pass an STD on to her? What changes would you need to make?

As a young man who is not sleeping with his girlfriend, what advice would you give to your peers on what is keeping you in sexual integrity?

GOD'S FORGIVENESS

When Jesus saw their faith, he said, "Friend, your sins are forgiven."
—Luke 5:20

Anytime we talk about *obeying* God, it is very important that you also understand the *forgiveness* of God. So often when we sin, the guilt or condemnation sits so heavily on us that we feel we can't ever get things right again with God. What we know in our heads about His forgiveness, we can't seem to transfer to our hearts and really receive that forgiveness. So I want to take the time to give you as much ammunition as I can to teach you how to forgive yourself and others.

> *He who conceals his sins does not prosper, but whoever confesses and renounces them finds mercy.* —Proverbs 28:13

If you have fallen to sexual sin or sexual activity of any kind—and this includes impure thoughts/fantasies that can grow into monsters in your mind in no time—there is forgiveness with God.

Now I'm not talking about the kind of cheap grace where we ask for forgiveness, knowing full well we will be doing it again next weekend. I'm talking about the forgiveness that has repentance all over it.

Repentance is a 180-degree turn to walk away from *everything* that has to do with that situation and let God clean your heart, mind, and spirit over the matter. An alcoholic, as he is getting free from that addiction, does not hang out in bars. He can't, or he'll fall back into it in no time. You must walk away, no matter how hard it may be. This is not easy to do. But in most situations it is necessary to walk away.

REPENTANCE IS A 180-DEGREE TURN TO WALK AWAY

SEEK HIS FREEDOM

If you are serious with God, and you want the "plans He has for you," then I am sure He would say to you, **"Where I am taking you, my son, that sin cannot come with us."** You must rid yourself of every hindrance that will keep you from the destiny God has for you. God knows your heart. He will move heaven and earth to help you. But you need to make it your desire.

You can be clean again. It is a process, but you wouldn't believe the freedom that can come to you if you begin to speak certain Scriptures over your life. We will talk about these Scriptures below.

You see, the enemy of your soul wants you to remain in a pit that you can't get out of. He wants you to feel so condemned in what you have done that you won't even seek the freedom that you could have. If he can hold you down, then you won't be effective for the kingdom of God or become the man/warrior within, and that is his goal for you.

The enemy is banking on the fact that when you have sinned in any way, you will stop your communication with God. This prevents you from praying, and then he has his hooks in you, keeping you separated from the One who has your very answer in the palm of His hand.

SPEAK HIS WORD

Here are a few Scriptures that you can write on 3x5 cards and say out loud to yourself:

If we confess our sins, He is faithful and just and will forgive us our sins and cleanse us from all unrighteousness. —1 John 1:9

Who is a God like you, who pardons sin and forgives the transgression of the remnant of his inheritance? You do not stay angry forever but delight to show mercy. You will again have compassion on us; you will tread our sins underfoot and hurl all our iniquities into the depths of the sea. —Micah 7:18-19

But you, O Sovereign Lord, deal well with me for Your name's sake; out of the goodness of Your love, deliver me. For I am poor and needy, and my heart is wounded within me. —Psalm 109:21-22

Wash me thoroughly from my iniquity and cleanse me from my sin. Purify me with hyssop and I shall be clean; wash me, and I shall be whiter than snow. —Psalm 51:2, 7

You can be sure that, in time, you will start to feel clean again because you are clean by the work Christ did at Calvary. I am telling you, gentlemen, there is nothing, *nothing* that is more freeing than a clear, clean sound mind. It gives you peace and confidence, and opens you up to hear the voice of God for yourself. Your whole walk will change.

GOD RESTORES

The Lord is so good. He is so faithful to restore us back. Think of the story of the woman caught in adultery in John 8:3-11. Jesus didn't yell at her, He didn't ignore her, He didn't make her feel awful about her sin. He didn't condemn her, accuse her, or judge her. He simply, lovingly took her by the hand, lifted her to her feet and forgave her...**but** He gave her instructions after He forgave her...to go and sin no more.

Can you imagine how this woman felt? Scared to death I'm sure, naked in the middle of the street with those who wanted to stone her, were gawking at her, trying to trip Jesus up so that they would have grounds to accuse Him. Yet Jesus, in the same heroic way that a Prince might rescue His bride, chose to challenge those who were accusing her.

Remember, he challenged that whoever among them was without sin should be the one to throw the first stone at her. He chose to publicly rescue the one who was laughed at, gawked at, and accused. Only a Savior does that. And when He asked her to go and sin no more, it was to let her know this is not how she was to live her life anymore. She was forgiven. She was to be cherished and treated with dignity, not going around to other men's beds to find her self-worth or false love.

HE SAYS TO YOU, as He reaches out His hand to lift you back on your feet again, "You Are Forgiven". Stay out of the grasp of young girls' beds; it is not His plan for you. Instead, He has someone who will love you as He does, who will be an extension of His love for you. It is through the commitment of marriage that you will have this kind of relationship that He desires for you. All that the world offers you outside the marriage bed is a false love, a false way to express that love, and an unworthiness of heart and character that He would never want you to carry as His son.

I just read this today. It is perfect for what we are talking about. Grab a hold of this...in fact, write it on the tablet of your heart..."The enemy wants to define you by your scars. Jesus wants to define you by His." Louie Giglio

"YOU ARE FORGIVEN".

NO CONDEMNATION

Condemnation is what students have told me they struggle with the most. After falling to sin of any kind, feelings of guilt and condemnation can be so overwhelming. Condemnation is not from God; it is a trick from the enemy to lie to you that you are not forgiven.

Isn't it funny how the enemy is the first to tell you what you are doing is no big deal, but then he is the first to condemn you for it after you have taken the bait.

Condemning thoughts rob a person of forgiveness. They are deceptive thoughts of the enemy. Lies that he wants to use to trap you. Once again the truth says, *"There is therefore now, **no condemnation** for those who are in Christ Jesus."* (Romans 8:1 NASB)

If you have confessed your heart to the Lord, you are in Christ, therefore there is no condemnation. God convicts us of our sin so He can draw us to Himself, but He never condemns us.

When you hear that voice of condemnation, you must know that is *not* the Lord speaking like that to you. Phrases like: "You are so stupid, you know better," "You will never be forgiven for that," "God can't possibly use you now," "You hypocrite, look what you have done and you are telling others to be sexually pure." Do those sound familiar? Condemnation is not from God. He convicts, the enemy condemns. That's a huge difference. Satan is always trying to draw you away from God. You cannot believe the lie, you must recognize it quickly so as not to be drawn in and dragged into a pit.

CONDEMNATION IS NOT FROM GOD.

The Lord looks right through you and is not angry or ashamed of what you may have done or who you are. He is calling you to be serious about your change of heart. He wants you to accept His forgiveness, repent, forgive yourself, and trust that what He said, He will do. You are whiter than snow the moment you confess your sin. He remembers it no more.

God will not forsake a broken spirit or a broken heart…He says in Psalm 51:17 that *"My sacrifice, O God, is a broken spirit; a broken and contrite heart you, God, will not despise."* He will cleanse you. You will feel whole again. He is for you and not against you. He isn't mad *at* you, He is mad *about* you. Remember: God convicts—the enemy condemns. You are forgiven.

THE GOD OF THE SECOND CHANCE

God is absolutely the God of the second chance. He gives us endless times to get things right. Often when the decision has been made to have sex and then there is regret afterward, teens seem to think, "Well I already did it so what's the use, I might as well continue." That is a lie and a way to stay in the pit much longer than you ever wanted to.

When you make the commitment to a second chance, you are saying that you have made a clear decision that you will take the opportunity to wait until you say I do at the altar. God can and has restored thousands of those who chose to abstain after having already participated in sexual activity, making their wedding night brand new.

Remember sex is not just physical, it is emotional, spiritual, and mental —the whole person. The Lord can and does completely restore all of that back to you and desires to do so. He has honored many of those who have chosen to recommit this area of their lives back to Him.

THE LORD IS WAITING FOR YOU

Why not start today. Why not make a commitment to lay all of this at the feet of Jesus, and to run with Him a free man. You must be determined. You are going on with all the Lord has for you. Make a decision: I will be a clean man of God. I am not going back. That is my commitment.

Now I didn't say a perfect man of God. I said a clean. That means God knows that you are willing and trying to walk in obedience. You need His help to do so. Ask Him to guide you through this freedom….He has not asked you to do this on your own. Trust Him. Use His Word…Trust it is there to cleanse you. Ask others to walk with you. You are forgiven…He is waiting for you like the father waiting on the prodigal son to come home. *"When he saw him a long way off, the father ran to the son and welcomed him home."* (Luke 15:11-32) That is what the Father does when you come running home to Him. No condemnation…no yelling at you. He will run to you. He is waiting to forgive you and set you free.

> *He does not treat us as our sins deserve or repay us according to our iniquities. For as high as the heavens are above the earth, so great is His love for those who fear Him; as far as the east is from the west, so far has He removed our transgressions from us.* —Psalm 103:10-12

FORGIVING OTHERS

I realize it is very hard to forgive someone who has hurt you terribly. Sometimes painfully hard. But forgiving others for whatever they may have done is the only way you will remain free in heart and spirit. God wants to release you from holding onto the hurt. You want to avoid bitterness, jealousy, being offended all the time, anger, frustration, selfishness, and self-pity at all cost. These are the consequences of not forgiving someone, of holding a grudge because you think they deserve it.

This will hurt no one but you. You hold yourself in bondage when you don't forgive. You hold yourself hostage, a prisoner of your own making. The other person may be freely doing their thing, but you are churning inside because you have gone over this time and time and time again in your mind, and now all of those feelings have grown into monsters over your thought life. You are not even yourself anymore because now you want to get even or make the other person feel just as bad as they made you feel.

I was angry with someone for 10 years—read that again…10 years—over a matter that was devastating to me. Who do you think got the worst of that situation, me or them? Me! When I recognized the fact that I had no right to hold someone captive in my heart like that and that vengeance was not mine but God's, and released it to Him, I was finally free.

If you have hurt someone, you must take the initiative to go and apologize and make it right with that person. You can say that you forgive a friend, but if you shun that person and remove them from your life, you haven't forgiven them from your heart. You also must forgive the girls who have sinned with you in pre-marital sex.

> *For if you forgive men for their transgressions, your heavenly Father will also forgive you. But if you do not forgive men, then your Father will not forgive your transgressions.* —Matthew 6:14-15 (NASB)

THE POISON OF UNFORGIVENESS

Unforgiveness destroys relationships. It causes marriages to end, friendships to part, siblings to stop talking to one another, etc. It is meant to divide and not unite. It is a dangerous hold against someone.

It is the same thing in forgiving yourself. You may have done things that you haven't told a single soul. You may have been involved in sexual sin, or you may be right now while you are reading this. Maybe your girlfriend had an abortion and none of your friends know. Or maybe it's something altogether different, but you're thinking that no one will respect you anymore if they knew. You have learned to hide things, keeping them in the dark. That can slowly eat away at every fiber of your heart and spirit.

In not forgiving yourself, all you are doing is fueling the fire of the enemy, because he knows he can trick you into believing that you have overplayed your hand and now there is no way that God will forgive what you have done. The enemy will make you hold yourself captive, hiding in bondage as a hostage. It's a slow death grip. And when you choose not to forgive yourself or others, you are simply saying to God, "Your sacrifice wasn't good enough. Your blood wasn't powerful enough to make me whole again."

> *But God says to you, "Come now, let us reason together. Though your sins are as scarlet, they will be as white as snow; though they are red like crimson, they will be like wool."* —Isaiah 1:18 (NASB)

THE ENEMY WILL MAKE YOU
HOLD YOURSELF CAPTIVE

ACCEPT GOD'S FORGIVENESS

Let yourself off the hook and accept and receive God's forgiveness. It is time to look up, grab hold of His hands that are reaching to you, and let Him lift you back on your feet again. He never made you to live in the pig pen; He made you for the palace. Forgive yourself. He does—and that's the best place to start.

May this prayer help to restore your soul. Say it out loud to yourself until it gets into your heart.

> Heavenly Father, forgive me for all my sins. Let the power of Your blood wash away every sin, guilt, and shame from me. Wash away even the memories of them from my mind. For I know they are waging war against my soul. Help and guide me in Your truth and teach me all things that pertain to godliness, purity, and true holiness. Thank You for your mercies that are new every morning. Help me to see myself the way You see me, free and blameless before You. Thank You for washing me and making me whiter than snow. I receive and believe Your love and forgiveness for me. In Jesus's name I pray. Amen.

LOOK ONE MORE TIME!

I pray that this helps you understand the importance of forgiving yourself and trusting the mercy of God and His grace over you. *"Mercy triumphs over judgement"* (James 2:13). You can start again. The Lord will take your heart and with His compassion fill you again with the cleansing power of His love. He wants you free from everything that has held you captive. There is not one thing you have done that He would turn His back or separate you from His love. That is not the God we serve. The Lord has purposed you to be a man of valor and integrity. He forgives and forgets. Jesus took the sin in our lives; He became that sin for our sake. We are not the sin we committed. He took it upon Himself to be that sin so we can be free. What mercy. What grace. What love.

The Lord has promised you in His Word,

> *...that neither death, nor life, nor angels, nor principalities, nor things present, nor things to come, nor powers, nor height, nor depth, now any*

other created thing, shall be able to separate us from the love of God, which is in Christ Jesus our Lord. —Romans 8:38–39 (NASB)

Make it a point to come to Him in the brokenness of your wounded heart. He will take that heart and restore it back to what He wanted it to be from the start. And you will enjoy a relationship with the Lord like you've never known.

WE ARE NOT THE SIN WE COMMITTED.

You need to also give this the time that is needed. If you don't feel forgiven right away that doesn't mean that you are not. If you don't feel like you have released that person you are holding unforgiveness toward, realize that will take time. Take it as an opportunity for reading His word for yourself, and memorizing Scriptures (like the ones I gave you in the above text), getting them deep in your heart. You will begin to sense His forgiving power in no time.

You are loved and you are forgiven. If you were the only one on the earth, He would have died just for you. Wrap your heart in that fact and enjoy the cleansing power of His love and mercy toward you.

IT'S YOUR TURN

Take the time to think about these questions from Chapter Seven. Your answers will help you in making clear and wise decisions for yourself. Don't skip this. This is your life. Take the time to make the changes in this area of sexual integrity.

JOURNAL: CHAPTER SEVEN

Do you believe God forgives you for anything and everything? Do you believe you can start over if you need to with sexual integrity?

Do you know how to receive God's forgiveness? Explain.

Does condemnation affect your response to God's forgiveness to you? Explain.

_____

_____

_____

_____

_____

_____

Is there someone you need to forgive that you just are having too difficult of a time forgiving? Write out those feelings. At least get them onto paper. Actually it is a good thing to write that person a letter. Not sending it to them, but write it all out, the hurt and pain and then give it to God. Take the time to write out those feelings. You deserve to be free from anything that is choking the life out of you through unforgiveness.

_____

_____

_____

_____

_____

_____

_____

Why would unforgiveness be a poison to you?

TAKE ACTION:

Write a letter to the Lord, first asking Him for forgiveness in any area of sexual immorality that you may have been involved with and thanking Him for His cleansing power and love to help you start anew as you continue to mature and grow. Those who are walking strong in this area already, thank Him for that strength as you also continue to mature and grow.

I pray you strengthen your commitment to sexual integrity. Surrender what needs to be placed at His feet, and trust Him to bring all things together in its time. Set boundaries that you are willing to make for yourself and the Lord until you say "I do" at the altar. Give Him this area of your life of love, sex and relationships. He knows what He is doing. Trust Him.

THE ARMOR OF GOD

Finally, be strong in the Lord and in the strength of His might. Put on the full armor of God, so that you will be able to stand firm against the schemes of the devil.
—Ephesians 6:10-11 (NASB)

I couldn't have a book entitled *The Warrior Within* without having the final chapter about the armor of God. When I was a teacher at a private Christian school in Pittsburgh, I had the high school Bible classes learn these six pieces of the armor and told them they will need them their whole lives. Twenty years later, former students are still telling me that they put the armor on every day and have taught it to their kids. You see when you realize you are in a war with an enemy that wants to deceive and lie to you and to steal all God has in store for you, you better know what kind of armor you need to come against that spiritual enemy!

We are all in this together. As believers in Jesus, we have an enemy that fires deadly shots daily at each of us. This segment is not to glorify Satan, it's to expose him for who he is. That he is a liar and the father of lies. There is never any truth in him. He is a deceiver and will do anything to throw you off your course that Jesus has for you. Jesus had to deal with him, you and I will have to deal with him. You may have seen the movie **Gladiator.** General Maximus shouts at one point, "Stay together! As one!" You are not in this battle alone. You are surrounded by a great cloud of witnesses. It's time he is exposed and you know who you are fighting.

When you look at the Scripture above you see two words I want to zero in on. First of all, the apostle Paul would never have told us to put this armor on if he wasn't adamant that we had an enemy who is scheming to take us out of the plan of God and the victory He has for your life. And don't be mistaken, he will do whatever he needs to do to mess with you and take you out. When a warrior goes into battle, he must know who his enemy is and how to defeat him. You do not want to be ignorant and not realize where the deadly shots against you are coming from. Believe it or not, it is not from other people. It may seem that way, but it's not true. Look at the Scripture below.

For our struggle is not against flesh and blood, but against the rulers, against the powers, against the world forces in this darkness, against the spiritual forces of wickedness in the heavenly places.
—Ephesians 6:12

You are not, I repeat, *not* wrestling against flesh and blood…your parents, your friends, your brothers or sisters, your teachers, your co-worker, your coach, etc., they are not the enemy. You are wrestling against a spiritual force that wants nothing more than for you to shrink back and not be the man that God has called you to be. The enemy of your soul would love for you to believe that he is this character you see in cartoons, red devil with two horns. That is not the truth. I have heard people say, "I don't care if I go to hell one day, it just will be one big party." Oh, my friend, that is a lie from the very pit of hell. He is not your buddy or your friend. He is in the business to "steal, kill, and destroy" you. (See John 10:10.) It's time you recognize the influence he has over your life. He is a deceiver. We are going to pull back the veil in this segment and let the enemy know that we see what he is trying to do in our lives—that we are becoming wise to his schemes and that we have our eyes wide open.

YOU ARE WRESTLING AGAINST A SPIRITUAL FORCE

STAND FIRM AGAINST THE SCHEMES OF THE DEVIL.

1. **Stand Firm** – when you have done everything you know to do in prayer, in coming to God through His Word, in releasing it all to Him—keep standing. Many times the Lord has us wait longer than we would ever want to. But He sees the bigger picture in our lives. Our job is to trust and believe that He is working behind the scenes on our behalf. The Lord is the one who fights our battles. He knows exactly where you are. He vindicates, let Him. Your job is to stand—stand firm in the strength of His might. You are not standing alone.

2. **Schemes of the devil** – the devil is real. What does it make you feel like when you know someone is scheming against you? Purposefully watching your life, knowing your reactions to things, hiding so as not to be seen…scheming means a crafty or secret plan. Scheming specifically against you… your habits, your mistakes, your life. He figures out what entices you so he can trip you up. He is scheming. That should make you very angry. You are not wrestling against flesh and blood. You are wrestling against

powers and principalities of this dark world. It's time to have a scheme of your own.

God calls you a man of valor. Remember, valor means "the qualities of a hero; exceptional or heroic courage when facing danger (especially in battle)." Look at that! He calls you a mighty man of valor…He is with you and wants you to fight against that which is fighting against you. But you don't do this on your own. He is doing it alongside of you, with you and for you. You just need to recognize you are in a fight and stand and see Him battle on your behalf. Your part is to put your armor on and believe that the Lord is and will bring you through your battles. You may get bruised and wounded here and there. There are not too many wars when soldier's come out unscathed. But, you will have victory. And you will still be standing.

IT'S TIME TO HAVE A SCHEME OF YOUR OWN.

Therefore put on the full armor of God, so that when the day of evil comes, you may be able to stand your ground, and after you have done everything, to stand. Stand firm then, with the belt of truth buckled around your waist, with the breastplate of righteousness in place, and with your feet fitted with the readiness that comes from the gospel of peace. In addition to all this, take up the shield of faith, with which you can extinguish all the flaming arrows of the evil one. Take the helmet of salvation and the sword of the Spirit, which is the word of God.
—Ephesians 6:13-17

So let me give you these 6 pieces of the armor and their meaning – your job is to put them on daily along with the Scripture that goes with each piece. (*I took some of the information about the Roman armor from Christ-Centered Mail, Inc.)

Gird your loins with truth – The loins is the region of the hips, groin and lower abdomen. To gird them means to fasten or secure with a belt. When preparing for battle, a soldier would put on his belt first. The belt is designed to keep other pieces of the soldier's armor in place, including his sword. What is meant by "gird your loins" is that it's a call to be prepared. Paul related the belt to that of truth. To be firmly established in the truth of God's Word. God's Word is truth and therefore the foundation to all the other pieces of spiritual armor. You are kept free from the enemy's lies by abiding in God's truth.

Also, this involves not allowing deceit and unconfessed sin to separate you from fellowship with God. It also involves being a person of integrity. Satan attacks truth with lies. He especially focuses on attacking God's promises by casting doubt of God's goodness toward you. By abiding in the truth, walking in the truth, and speaking the truth, you will be spiritually ready in every circumstance.

I am the way, and the truth, and the life; no one comes to the Father but through Me. —John 14:6 (NASB)

Breast Plate of Righteousness – This piece covers your physical and spiritual heart. Your heart is your most vital organ. One shot to the heart would kill the soldier. This breastplate was designed and used to protect the soldier's heart. In understanding this as a piece of the armor of God —the breastplate of righteousness means you are called and chosen to live a free life in Christ. You are in right standing with Him. That's why the enemy takes shots at you. You create the environment whether you invite the Lord into your life and find the favor of God, or come out of alignment with God and invite the enemy to rule over you.

You must understand this. You can pray against the enemy's attacks on your life until you are literally blue in the face, but if you are not walking in the truth or ignoring the truth of God's word, you are pretty much wasting your breath. You are called to *"walk in a manner worthy of the calling by which you have been called"* (Ephesians 4:1 NASB). Those habits that have you captive, those people whose opinion you hold more than God's opinion about you, that drug that is confusing your mind...Christ's death on the cross washed away your sins and made you right with Him. This allowed the Holy Spirit to come and live within you. The Holy Spirit now gives you the life and power to live above sin. He imparts in you godly living. **This** is the breastplate of righteousness, a vital piece of the armor.

I am in right standing before God because of what Jesus has done for me.

Shod my feet with the preparation of the gospel of Peace – The sandals of the Roman soldiers were heavy sandals studded with nails to give a secure foothold to those who would stand firm. Having your feet planted so that you can hold your ground when the attacks come. Oh to walk in peace, His peace. These battle shoes purposely are used to give you peace that passes understanding. Simply meaning, you "trust in the Lord with all of your heart and do not lean on your own understanding." You dig your shoes in no matter how scary the circumstance and trust His Word.

I personally watched a friend, whose daughter was diagnosed with cancer at 13 years of age, dig her feet in, trust God through all her tears and fear, and find a peace above the circumstance. Her daughter is now cancer free. But I was experiencing the gospel in full view by watching her reaction to such a trying, heart wrenching time in her life.

Jesus is not haphazard with your life. He knows you. He cares. He sees you. He knows when you are in a place of anguish, fear, mistrust, discouragement, losing hope. He offers you Himself so that you stop and let His peace rest on you. The peace of the full gospel. It's not the world's rest, which so often is laced with anxiety. His rest is the one that makes you sense you are above your circumstances and that you know He has your situation and He has the answer.

JESUS IS NOT HAPHAZARD WITH YOUR LIFE.

Put these shoes on daily. Too many people do not know what it is like to walk in this peace and therefore get bombarded by heavy artillery from the enemy causing them great anxiety and unnecessary fear. Dig those shoes in daily.

Peace I leave with you, My peace I give to you. Not as the world gives do I Give to you. Let not your heart be troubled nor let it be fearful.
—John 14:27 (NASB)

The Shield of Faith – which you will be able to extinguish all the flaming arrows of the evil one – The Roman shield was a central part of the soldier's defense. It was rectangular in shape and rounded on the ends. It was typically made from two sheets of wood that were glued together, then covered with canvas and leather. The canvas and leather could be doused with water to protect against flaming arrows. Burning arrows were designed to stick to the shields and catch them on fire. The soldier carrying the shield was forced to cast it away and then became defenseless.

The shield weighed about 22 pounds and was roughly 37 to 42 inches high and 27 to 33 inches across. A metal piece ran across the center of the shield, so it could also be used as a weapon to punch or push forward. (The above information taken from lifehopeandtruth.com by David Johnson, 2018)

Paul, in his analogy of the Christian armor, says that "above all" the shield of faith should be raised. Paul mentions in Ephesians that the shield of faith is needed to defend against the attacks of Satan. The temptations of the wicked one are like these burning arrows. These arrows come in so many forms…evil thoughts strongly injected into the mind; words of: you're not good enough; you can't; you will never be a man; shame on you; what's the matter with you; you don't even have a dad, how would you know… and this can go on and on and on. The shield of faith is the armor God has given us to defend against those burning arrows. Jesus is our shield. And all of those fiery darts can bounce off of that shield as we lift up His name, His word against those fiery darts. Raise this shield daily. It's imperative.

With respect to the promises of God, I shall not waiver in unbelief but to stand firm. For whatever He has promised, He is able also to perform.
—Romans 4:20-21 (NASB)

The Helmet of Salvation - When a soldier puts on his armor, the helmet is the last piece of armor to go on. It is the final act of readiness in preparation for combat. A helmet is vital for survival. If the head is badly damaged, obviously the rest of the armor will be of little use.

Rather than guns and tanks, our weapons are those of the "full armor of God." This helmet of salvation helps you fight against every imagination, every stronghold, to take captive every thought that is against the knowledge of God. What is a stronghold? Any thought that holds you captive, that builds a thought process that makes it very difficult to break.

THE BATTLEFIELD OF THE MIND IS REAL.

Your enemy loves to mess with your mind, your head. Because of the blood of Jesus and the power of the cross, our enemy no longer has any hold on us. He knows that, but if we do not know that, and most Christians live like they don't, then he schemes and takes advantage of us. We all battle thoughts that simply are not true but sound like they are. The battlefield of the mind is real. That's why it is imperative that you use the Word of God against those thoughts and take them captive.

As you wear the helmet of salvation every day your mind becomes more insulated against the suggestions, schemes, desires and traps the enemy lays out for you. You choose to guard your mind and heart in Christ Jesus.

This Scripture will show you just what I am talking about by taking every thought captive.

Though I walk in the flesh, I do not war according to the flesh. For the weapons of my warfare are not of flesh, but they are powerful before God for the pulling down of strongholds. I am destroying imaginations, speculations and every lofty thing raised up against the knowledge of God. And I am taking every thought captive to the obedience of Christ. —2 Corinthians 10:3-6 (NASB)

This Scripture is showing you and challenging you that you do not war according to the flesh. You have the authority, in God's Word, to take those thoughts and imaginations captive.

Look what it says, those thoughts are raised up against the knowledge of God. So whatever negative thought that comes through your mind, you have the ability to weigh it against what Christ would think. Words of discouragement, hopelessness, suicide, lust, you're a failure, condemnation etc. Those are NOT from the Lord. They are not His thoughts toward you. That's why you must be aware of those thoughts and then scheme against them with the Word of God. This battle is a winnable war because of the power of the cross. You need to know your enemy, your opponent, and scheme against his tactics.

The Sword of the Spirit which is the Living Word of God – The sword used by Roman soldiers was known as a gladius; and in the hands of a skilled man, it was a fearsome weapon. It was sharpened on both sides, making it lethal as it cuts and slices everyway you wield it. The sword is the only offensive weapon in the armor. So using this weapon against your enemy is everything you need.

If you have noticed, everything I am trying to explain to you throughout this entire book, I always refer you to the Word of God. Why? Because it is *"living and active and sharper than any two-edged sword"* (Hebrews 4:19). So that is telling me that it cuts and slices every way you swing it. Every time you use it. Let me give you two Scriptures of proof of what the Word does for you:

> For the word of God is living and active and sharper than any two-edged sword, and piercing as far as the division of soul and spirit of both joints and marrow, and able to judge the thoughts and intentions of the heart.   —Hebrews 4:12 (NASB)

Look at this Scripture and what the Word of God does when you use it...

It's living and active. Guys it's alive because it is God breathed. When God breathed and spoke over the earth it came alive. When you speak His word over your situation, it comes alive and it becomes active over your life.

Sharper than any two-edged sword. It cuts through every question you have. The enemy is afraid of the Word because he knows it works. Look, he even used it himself, twisting it, when tempting Jesus in the wilderness. But Jesus came right back at him with the Word saying, "it is written." The enemy knows the Word of God because he knows the power it will be over your life.

Piercing soul and spirit; joints and marrow. The Word is powerful to cut and slice through physical, emotional, and spiritual brokenness. It literally transforms lives.

Able to judge the thoughts and intentions of the heart. Look at this, guys... the Word is so cutting and powerful that it will show you when your thoughts are wrong or your intentions are wrong. He is so for you. He wants you on the right course He has for your life. So often we don't even know our own heart...but He does.

> O LORD, you have searched me, and you know me. You know when I sit down and when I stand up, You understand my thoughts before I think them. You are acquainted with all my ways. There is not a word that I speak, but you know it completely. Such knowledge is too awesome for me, it is high I cannot attain it. —Psalm 139:1-4

Look how much he knows you. He. Knows. You. His word is your greatest offensive and defensive weapon in this battle for your heart.

Look at one more Scripture to prove the point about God's Word:

> All Scripture is inspired by God and profitable for teaching, for reproof, for correction, for training in righteous; so that the man of God may be adequate, equipped for every good work. —2 Timothy 3:16-17 (NASB)

That is such a great Scripture. It just reiterates what the power of His Word will do for you when you speak it over your life. And guys, it's not enough to memorize or meditate on it, you must believe that it is so. If you put this into practice and use His Word as a wielding two-edged sword, you will live a life of great victory! You are so valued in His eyes that this battle is worth fighting.

Greater is He that is in you than he that is in the world.

—1 John 4:4

No weapon formed against me shall prosper. —Isaiah 54:17

LOOK ONE MORE TIME

As the last chapter of this book, the Armor of God is your defense against the enemies schemes over your life. This chapter of the study is probably the most crucial for you to be able to walk out this whole concept of "young men staying strong in a reckless world." Knowing the Lord in an intimate way and having a relationship with Him on a daily basis will help you make wise and confidant choices for yourself when choosing friends, where to go to college, a career, who to date, marry and so many more decisions in life. Being able to walk in the authority and power of the Word of God simply because you have taken the time to get to know your Creator personally will change the direction of your life completely. This is a life style, not just something you commit to do for a week or so. This is something you do for the rest of your days here on earth. Make your quiet time and the armor of God part of your life. I am a witness to all that God will do in a life that seeks Him first before anything else.

I want Ryan's words of encouragement to send you off on this journey you are called to. He has so many good things to leave you with:

The world is all about immediate self-gratification. Whether it is food, entertainment, success, a house, or a family, everyone wants the "American Dream" and they want it now. The problem for young men is that they are overwhelmed with so many ideas that directly contradict God's Word. The same battles that you are facing in high school are some of the same battles that you face as an adult. They may look different, but it's the same battle for your heart.

Having been through, and still going through, this battle, I can say that having a strong biblical foundation is essential to your fight against the world. If you are waiting to be attacked by lust, greed, anger or anything else the world throws at you, then you are already losing the battle. Go on the offensive. Memorize Scripture to use in times of temptation. Set boundaries for what type of friends you are going to let influence your life. Be uncompromising on staying pure before marriage. You need to make this decision before you ever go out with friends or a girl, so that you are not caught off guard by your emotions. By forming these types of God honoring habits when you are young, you will not have years of regret hanging over you as you move into marriage and kids.

I want to encourage you in something. No one gets it right all of the time, so if you do stumble in any one of these areas, get back up, repent, and move past it. Do not let Satan keep you down because of failure. For years I was letting Satan hold me back because of choices I made in college. One of my BIGGEST and FREEING victories was reading Romans 8:1, *"Therefore, there is now no condemnation for those who are in Christ Jesus."* God opened my eyes that He had forgiven me so it was time to forgive myself. Since then, the struggles that I face don't hold me back. I move forward to finish the race that I have started.

Ryan

A STRONG BIBLICAL FOUNDATION IS ESSENTIAL TO YOUR FIGHT AGAINST THE WORLD.

You were called to make a stand for your generation, even if you have to stand alone. You are a young man chosen by God to live in this generation. You have been called to live an extraordinary life, one that will change your generation. You can lead the pack. You can bring your friends with you… you have a voice. Live your life out loud!

Trust Him…He is for you! You have a battle set before you and you have the tools to fight that battle through your private and personal quiet time and with the armor of God.

The LORD set apart the godly for himself. The LORD will answer when I call to him. —Psalm 4:3

IT'S YOUR TURN

*Take the time to think about these questions from Chapter Eight.
Your answers will help you in making clear and wise decisions for
yourself. Don't skip this. This is your life. Take the time to make the
changes in this area of sexual integrity.*

JOURNAL: CHAPTER EIGHT

In putting on the armor daily, there is no piece for your back, why do you
think that is?

Knowing that the enemy is scheming against you as stated in Ephesians 6,
what does that mean to you? And how does that effect the way you see the
battles over your life?

In the material given to you in this chapter, it's time to have a scheme of your own against the enemy of your soul. Write out what that means to you and how you can begin.

_____

_____

_____

_____

_____

_____

_____

_____

The Sword of the Spirit is represented as the Living Word of God. Wield that sword, gentlemen; it's invaluable to you to know the Word in your heart. Write out three Scriptures that are familiar to you and speak them out loud to the Lord over your life in prayer.

_____

_____

_____

_____

_____

_____

_____

_____

TAKE ACTION:

Here are my final questions to you after going through this entire book. Do you believe that God wants to use you for your generation? Do you want to be used by God for your generation? If so, in what ways? After you write your answer, take it to the Lord in prayer.

Do you see the importance of sexual integrity after reading this material? How?

Do you trust God with the plans He has for you? If so, in what ways are you trusting Him?

FINAL WORD

Congratulations, you have just finished this eight part study on how to stand strong in a culture spinning out of control. With integrity, strength, and certainty, I pray you make a decision of a life time to do this relationship thing with the girl of your heart, as God has set it up for you and for your joy and pleasure. I commend you because not many of your peers are hearing this kind of truth through the Word of God. They are still lost in their thinking and their actions.

I trust that giving you the tools within this book will help you to have the confidence you need as you finish out your high school and college years.

I know that you are under a lot of pressure from the voices of the world that make fun of those who choose sexual integrity or who choose to start over again. It takes great courage to stand up against the crowd. But you are not alone. This is why I purposely put in here a few testimonies of guys who have gone before you. I hope they give you courage, whether you have fallen or not, to keep moving forward. The Lord will honor your love life when the right time comes. Trust Him with that, He knows what He is doing.

So now it's up to you. You have a choice to make. It is your choice. A "5-second decision." No one can make it for you. My greatest prayer for you is that you make a choice to follow the Lord with all of your heart. To value and use self-control above the noise of the crowd. Remember, you have a great future ahead of you with the girl the Lord has chosen for you. He promises that there is an appointed time for everything under the sun. Give Him time and wait on Him. He is not haphazard with your life. Trust Him. He knows you better than you know yourself.

Thank you for giving me the opportunity to talk with you so candidly on this subject. May you share the hope with others. Be that *Warrior Within* that will change the course of your generation!

God's richest blessings to you always!
Luanne

The angel of the LORD appeared to him and said to him,
"The LORD is with you, O valiant warrior."
—Judges 6:12

WWW.LUANNEBOTTA.COM